❋ A Course in Happiness ❋

A Course in Happiness

Mastering the 3 Levels
of Self-Understanding That Lead to
True and Lasting Contentment

MARDI HOROWITZ, M.D.

JEREMY P. TARCHER/PENGUIN
a member of Penguin Group (USA) Inc.
New York

JEREMY P. TARCHER/PENGUIN
Published by the Penguin Group
Penguin Group (USA) Inc., 375 Hudson Street, New York, New York 10014, USA •
Penguin Group (Canada), 90 Eglinton Avenue East, Suite 700, Toronto, Ontario M4P 2Y3,
Canada (a division of Pearson Canada Inc.) • Penguin Books Ltd, 80 Strand,
London WC2R 0RL, England • Penguin Ireland, 25 St Stephen's Green,
Dublin 2, Ireland (a division of Penguin Books Ltd) • Penguin Group (Australia),
250 Camberwell Road, Camberwell, Victoria 3124, Australia (a division of Pearson
Australia Group Pty Ltd) • Penguin Books India Pvt Ltd, 11 Community Centre,
Panchsheel Park, New Delhi–110 017, India • Penguin Group (NZ),
67 Apollo Drive, Rosedale, North Shore 0632, New Zealand
(a division of Pearson New Zealand Ltd) • Penguin Books (South Africa)
(Pty) Ltd, 24 Sturdee Avenue, Rosebank, Johannesburg 2196, South Africa

Penguin Books Ltd, Registered Offices: 80 Strand, London WC2R 0RL, England

Most Tarcher/Penguin books are available at special quantity discounts for bulk purchase for
sales promotions, premiums, fund-raising, and educational needs. Special books or book excerpts
also can be created to fit specific needs. For details, write Penguin Group (USA) Inc. Special
Markets, 375 Hudson Street, New York, NY 10014.

Library of Congress Cataloging-in-Publication Data

Horowitz, Mardi Jon, date.
A course in happiness : mastering the 3 levels of self-understanding that lead
to true and lasting contentment / Mardi Horowitz.
p.   cm.
Includes bibliographical references and index.
ISBN 978-1-58542-694-2
1. Happiness.   2. Contentment.   I. Title.
BF575.H27H66   2009   2008042053
158—dc22

Printed in the United States of America
1   3   5   7   9   10   8   6   4   2

BOOK DESIGN BY NICOLE LAROCHE

While the author has made every effort to provide accurate telephone numbers and Internet
addresses at the time of publication, neither the publisher nor the author assumes any responsibility for errors, or for changes that occur after publication. Further, the publisher does not have any
control over and does not assume any responsibility for author or third-party websites or their
content.

For Renée, with love,
and in memory of
Carol Horowitz and Aubrey Metcalf,
who also taught me a great deal about happiness

CONTENTS

Introduction 1

If you're happy and you know it, clap your hands.

I love this nursery school song. It brings a smile to my face and lifts my spirits every time I hear it. The simple lyrics and catchy tune teach small children the important skill of recognizing and acknowledging good feelings within themselves. For adults, getting in touch with a sense of happiness is rarely so simple—and achieving a lasting happiness can be extremely elusive or unattainable no matter how much it may appear that someone "has it all."

For more than forty years as a psychiatrist in private practice and as a professor of psychiatry at the University of California, San Francisco, I've worked with thousands of individuals as they've searched for greater meaning and happiness in their lives. While some struggled to heal from terrible tragedies and conditions and to recover a zest for living, many others strived simply to master the ordinary stresses of life or grappled to understand a mystifying, underlying discontent.

Through the years, I've met countless people who have had all the outward manifestations of success yet were still searching for the "golden key" that would unlock the secret to enduring inner satisfaction. What I have found is that there is no "golden key" to the achievement of happiness; there is only the hard work of creating the type of inner peace that underlies it. And what is the raw material from which this inner peace is built? In a word: *self-knowledge.* To grasp who we *are* and what is most important to us in this life.

There is an old saying that the mind is like a muscle: With exercise, it can build both strength and skill, and, with exercise, it can lead us to happiness. Putting our internal house in order can be hard work, but it is the most important work of all.

With this book I invite you to make the choice to see all that lies within you, to believe that you can have a heart full of peace and a happy life no matter what your history or your current circumstances or what may be awaiting you in your future. I'm not saying your life will be always blissful or problem free. I *am* saying that you can find a stable, serene center within yourself and live a life that you can honestly label as wonderful.

THE ROAD TO SELF-DISCOVERY

This book is comprised of a series of lessons, a virtual course in the achievement of happiness. Lesson by lesson, step by step, it will introduce you to a process of thinking about yourself, your goals, and your choices. Along the way, I will share with you stories of individuals who have turned their lives around through the hard work of self-analysis and self-directed change. And I will present exercises that will help you develop the skills to maintain a determined focus on what is really important to you—even when life throws you a curve ball.

When you make your mind a better tool for performing the crucial adult task of seeing yourself and your place in the world in sharp, undistorted focus, you arrive at fresh, clear ideas. You know the difference between fantasy and reality. You make good decisions. You're aware and accepting of your oh-so-human imperfections and the traps that can snare you. You free yourself of avoidances, inaccuracies, false assumptions, rationalizations, and projections. You take responsibility for goals, priorities, and all of your choices and actions.

It's a serious task to undertake this self-development, significant inner change requires hard effort. New patterns of behavior will always feel awkward at first, but practice creates familiarity. Through repetition, a new way of acting in the world can soon become your automatic style. Your poise and confidence will grow. So will your sense of satisfaction with life and your self-esteem, and you'll be establishing the strong foundation that will withstand whatever the winds of fate may blow your way.

The strategies that I will teach you have evolved from my work with patients who have succeeded at courageously exploring their inner landscapes, battling their demons, and growing in integrity, wisdom, and character. For some, the roadblock to serenity was unresolved past traumas or unsettling childhood memories or, conversely, struggles with anxious fantasies of an anticipated crisis. For others, resistance to thinking about difficult emotional issues and a lack of self-understanding were the obstacles preventing them from enjoying lives rich in meaning and fulfillment. For still others, the barrier to equanimity was a type of behavioral pattern, such as procrastination, perfectionism, severe self-criticism, selfishness, self-righteousness, indecisiveness, and wishful thinking, among others. When my patients gained more self-awareness and experienced the exhilaration of growing and changing, they found a renewed lust for life and a greater, steadfast inner peace.

As I observed my patients working so hard, drawing on great depths of courage and strength, I marveled at the healing, growth, and remarkable changes in their lives. Their discoveries and insights, the course of their journeys, are the knowledge I wish to pass on.

What are the core processes of creating a happy life? What are the dimensions of our identities as human beings? What gives our lives passion, purpose, and value? What are our deepest commitments and the ground from which our actions spring? How can we become more loving, wise, and joyful?

The answers to these questions are the message of *A Course in Happiness.*

TELLING MY TRUTH

In my own life, I know what it is to struggle with decisions, to be befuddled by choices, to long for personal happiness and yet be unsure about how to achieve it. I grew up in Hollywood, California, but stardust did not cover me. My parents were lower-middle-class working people. For the first ten years of my life, I was an only child, and I was very close to my mother and father. One of their highest priorities was for me to be well educated. They dreamed that I would go to college, find a professional calling, and have a good, stable, and secure life. I embraced that vision and applied myself to learning. I had high hopes that my future would unfold beautifully, although my notions of how this might come about were somewhat foggy.

I attended college at UCLA and then started medical school at the University of California, San Francisco. It was a tense time for me. I was full of insecurity, anxious about the competition, and doubtful of my ability to measure up to what would be required of me. It turned out that I earned high marks, and by the end of my first year of med school I felt much more confident as a student. But my social life was a different matter.

A few months earlier, I'd had a girlfriend who'd given me the ultimatum "Marry me or break up." I knew I wasn't ready for marriage, so I opted to break up, although it left me feeling quite dejected. I soon started dating another young woman but quickly discovered that she was seeing someone besides me. This ruffled my feathers a lot—I expected exclusivity—so I gave her an ultimatum, and, to my surprise and dismay, she chose the other guy.

Feeling betrayed, I felt I had to get away. Luckily, my

summer months between the first and second year of medical school were free, but I had little money and my options were limited. Then fate handed me the perfect solution: a job in Alaska with the U.S. Fish and Wildlife Service. For two months, I would guard five salmon streams from poachers, stationed alone on a remote, uninhabited bay in the northern wilderness.

Never mind that the only wilderness I'd ever known was the Hollywood Hills or that I'd never lived anywhere without traffic, neighbors, entertainment venues, and convenience shopping. Like many twenty-one-year-olds, I regarded myself as indestructible, and I viewed life as infinite. So off I went to become an enforcement officer, protecting the fish of Alaska.

The isolation turned out to be extremely difficult for me. It wasn't long before I began to think I'd made a terrible mistake. Marooning myself in the Alaskan wilderness may have been one of the most poorly considered decisions I'd ever made. I'd taken the job on impulse, as a way to escape feelings of disappointment and betrayal. Those reasons soon seemed pretty weak and immature. As well—I had to admit it—I was totally unsuited for the job. It gave me no personal satisfaction or fulfillment.

Yet, I had made a commitment, and I was stuck. During the time that I remained in Alaska, I faced truths about myself and gained insights that later became profoundly important to me. In the years to come, this self-knowledge would inform many of my choices. Throughout this book, I'll discuss further my process of self-exploration and discovery. From my own experiences and those of others, I will illustrate how when bad things happen, no matter how big or small, there is always an accompanying potential for growth and then for greater happiness than before.

After my Alaskan summer, I returned to San Francisco for my second year of medical school with a new conviction that I was where I belonged. It wasn't long before I began to consider if psychiatry—a field of medicine that deals with the intricacies of the psyche and the passages of life—could be the personal path to my fulfillment. At this time, I also met a lovely physical therapist, and we married. So there were other rewards for me as well.

Eventually, I made the choice to specialize in psychiatry, and as a psychiatric resident, I learned to listen as empathically as I could to the emotional pain of others and to be aware of my own feelings. The big lesson was how to "be with others" with compassion but without absorbing their helplessness and hopelessness. It required a great deal of attention to my own inner world and continuing personal growth.

Throughout my career, which started in the navy, where I treated military personnel who'd had traumatic experiences, I've explored how people handle stress, catastrophes, and loss, and how they can change and grow from the experience. Not everyone suffers from deeply damaging traumas, but all of us experience plenty of stress, and we can all gain from it. Anyone with a genuine willingness for self-exploration and self-improvement can build a more solid inner foundation and create a more vibrant, harmonious, and contented life.

FINDING CLARITY

In youth, all of us view the world through a distorted prism. That's the nature of childhood. Unlucky kids—those who were hurt by tragic events, damaged by emotional or physical abuse, or struggled with hardships—tend to see the world through an overly pessimistic lens, full of potential storms, dark and gray. Whereas lucky kids—those who enjoyed wonderful, protected, emotionally healthy childhoods—tend to view life through an overly optimistic lens. All they survey is rosy, full of sunshine and limitless opportunities.

As adults, we all need to find our way to realistic thinking. Clearing the mind of both excessive pessimism and excessive optimism is one of the central principles discussed in this book. If asked to choose, I'd say that over-optimism is the better weakness. A happy frame of mind fortifies morale and helps us cope. It is the way our species has survived. But a crystal-clear lens serves us best always and at any age.

As an expert in stress, trauma, and adult personality development, I'm familiar with every approach to psychotherapy. Research has shown the value of cognitive work to produce positive changes in the lives of many individuals. But research has also shown the key importance of the deeper sources within the psyche that establish a sense of solid balance, a coherence of self, and an ability to form significant and lasting attachment to others. To overcome unhappiness, it's necessary to change beliefs and thinking, and I fully appreciate the value of cognitive therapy in this respect. However, to achieve an enduring inner harmony, it's necessary to consider not just thinking patterns but all of the memories, fantasies, and emotions that go into creating the true "I" in each of us. The work must go deep, into the core of the self.

In this book, I will not be presenting a rehash of old psychoanalytic ideas. I will be introducing a contemporary integrative approach to therapy that corrects dysfunctional thinking, while increasing emotional stability, solidifying identity, strengthening the skills of maintaining close relationships with others, and encouraging maturity.

THE KEY PRINCIPLES

At the heart of this book is what I call the Three *I*s: Integration, Integrity, and Intimacy. These are the major pathways on the journey to knowing the self. At the foundation of deep, lasting human happiness, they are the three basic, vital, and interconnected cornerstones. These three *I* words define the essential components for achieving personal growth, effectively handling stress, gaining inner strength, sustaining emotional balance and stability, and maintaining equanimity in the face of life's ups and downs.

What do I mean by them?

Integration is the capacity to put together different aspects of the self. It involves assembling all of the pieces of a life story, clarifying emotional contradictions, and harmonizing aspirations and attitudes to establish a coherence that results in a whole, complete, understood, and respected "me."

Intimacy is the capacity to remain closely connected to relationships with family, friends, colleagues, and others in a social community, and it is crucial to achieving satisfaction with one's life. Intimacy combines sex with love and sharing with true give-and-take. At home, at work, and in the world at large, maintaining good, long-lasting relationships requires addressing the needs of self versus the needs of others, cooperation versus competition, and the issues of dependency, authority, and boundaries that shift as we age, our children grow up, our parents grow old, and all of our roles in the world evolve and change.

Integrity is the ability to know which values are most dear and which are lower in priority and then to be true to the most important ones even in the midst of conflict. It requires a high consciousness of self to harmonize competing values, but it is a skill that is indispensable in overcoming obstacles to achieving happiness.

This book will guide you in developing these qualities within yourself. But before we begin I would like to share with you a personal story that may give you some sense of how these personal strengths can help you to maintain inner peace even in the most difficult times.

OUT OF THE BLUE

Sometimes disaster strikes suddenly: cars collide, a fire ignites, a tornado touches down, a cancer is found, a horse throws a rider, or a terrorist attacks. Whatever the event, it changes our world forever. We all know this is possible. Until the phone rings with shattering news, or the police ring the doorbell, or a doctor delivers a dreaded diagnosis, we don't know how we'll respond.

It's not possible to be truly mentally prepared for devastating news, but it is possible to have a solid psychological foundation with which to withstand the blow. We are all subject to the whims of fate, but by virtue of our choices, we can pursue serenity rather than succumb to emotional chaos whenever possible.

In my own life, the first inkling of a looming disaster occurred suddenly one beautiful, sunny Saturday morning in January. My wife, Carol, and I were eating a leisurely breakfast when I looked across the table and saw an odd tinge of yellow in her eyes. She was wearing a bright turquoise blouse, so the hue wasn't a reflection of her clothing.

From my medical training, I knew this could be a symptom of something serious, and I felt the first twinge of concern. I reminded myself that it was too soon to jump to negative conclusions—a common reaction for almost everyone in an impending crisis—but I had a hard time controlling my rising anxiety and my spinning thoughts.

It took a few days and many tests before we knew what we were dealing with, and my worst fears were confirmed: The yellow in Carol's eyes turned out to be jaundice, the result of a blocked bile duct caused by a pancreatic cancer that had been silently progressing and was, by this time, advanced. Surgery was recommended, and we consented. Unfortunately, the results weren't what we'd hoped for, and the prognosis was grim. Carol was given less than six months to live. That's an estimate, we told each other, only an idea of what our medical team believes may happen; it's not necessarily true. We decided to try to stay as optimistic as possible while remaining realistic. We made many decisions about the best way to proceed. Carol started chemotherapy, hoping to hold back the cancer and increase her chances for surviving longer.

In the end, we had a little more than two years together before she lost her battle. Two years filled with meaningful conversations, many celebrations with family, and scores of other precious opportunities to make beautiful memories that I've stored and will cherish for the rest of my life. In the midst of our sadness, we were happy. I mean that. While facing the nightmare of terminal illness, knowing loss and terrible grief were inevitable, we still held on to our serenity. We couldn't lose it because our deep sense of fulfillment and inner harmony weren't dependent on external events; serenity came from within, where we had cultivated it through the years by identifying our values, establishing our intimacy, knowing who we were at the deepest levels of our beings, and knowing what was most important to us.

Throughout Carol's final illness, she and I were hurting intensely and terribly frightened, but we weren't paralyzed. Deep within, we were strong enough to cope, stick together, ride it out, and experience different kinds of happiness in the midst of our fear and grief.

Facing the facts about Carol's condition was a slow and difficult emotional journey for both of us. There were phases in the process. Sometimes, in the wee hours of the night, I felt like giving up, although there was nothing I could—or would—do that actually constituted giving up, but I knew that my feeling was temporary, a phase within a phase, and that it wasn't going to remain a constant state of mind. Carol and I had expected a much longer time together, and we each mourned the loss of that prospect.

Most of the time, we stayed in the present moment without trying to answer the inevitable question "Why is this happening to us?" which is, of course, unanswerable. We spent a lot of quiet time together. We talked about the five adult children we shared in our blended family and our hopes for their futures. We often held hands. We weren't morbid, and we didn't ignore death. Carol decided that she wanted to die at home, and she decided when she was ready for hospice care.

Two days before the hospice caretakers moved into our house, she and I went shopping for presents for our grandchildren. At the time, we had seven grandkids and a set of twins on the way. Although it hurt Carol to walk, she had fun deciding on the gifts. We stopped for tea at a little outdoor café. We reminisced. When our romance began, Carol had been a widow for ten years and I was divorced, but we'd been friends for a long time before that. Our friendship had always been the most important foundation of our relationship. We came home that afternoon with many bags full of children's toys and clothing and with hearts full of gratitude and contentment.

Again and again in my work I've seen that there can be extraordinary happiness even under the grimmest circumstances, and that afternoon I experienced it for myself. And later, as a widower, I reconfirmed another truth that I had often seen in my patients' lives: No story is without beauty and hope, even when it includes the wrenching loss of a beloved.

It takes courage, stamina, and inner work to hold on to equanimity in the face of events that bring the spirit close to the edge of despair. And although to some people this may sound Pollyannaish, through my work and my personal experience, I know it is a realistic, optimistic view, not an illusion. For young and old alike, thoughts and emotions rush into overdrive when a traumatic event occurs without warning. In the face of an unexpected new crisis, our minds tumble and spin in a rushing loop of images, often accompanied by pangs of painful emotion. These are not calm states of mind! Some spiritual philosophies, such as Zen Buddhism, and cognitive therapies that include mindfulness training are helpful for focusing on the present moment, without preoccupation with the past or worry about the future. Such mental discipline is valuable because it calms the mind.

When in crisis, recognizing that one's chaotic state of mind is temporary and getting beyond the spinning rut of pain are first priorities. Then the work of taking on difficult, stressful topics without being judgmental can begin, and new resolutions can be reached.

THE MAJOR TOOLS

As we move through the lessons in this book, I'll speak a lot about how to select one topic at a time for closer contemplation; how to examine all of your traits and experiences and assemble them into a whole, complete, and strong foundation of the authentic "you"; and how to examine your goals and reprioritize them.

I'll also explain how you can enhance your capacity for self-observation through what I refer to as the Five *R*s: Reconsider, Reperceive, Reappraise, Revise, and Rehearse. When you have a bird's-eye view of your thoughts and actions, you won't need to be led through psychotherapy by a licensed professional; you can be your own wise counsel. The Five *R*s are just one of the tools to help you examine yourself.

Another item in your tool box is the Three-Scenario Approach, a method of evaluating an emotionally fraught issue by looking at the most ideal, dreaded, and realistic outcomes to clarify your thinking. By first putting an idealized spin on a situation, then imagining a catastrophic outcome, and finally considering the most realistic appraisal, you'll be able to think more rationally, thereby increasing the likelihood of your making an appropriate future choice. I've illustrated this process throughout this book with several cases.

The Three-Time-Frames Technique is another strategy for expanding awareness. Simply put, by directing your thinking quite deliberately to the past, present, or future, you can design a new approach for handling issues in the now and create a more positive future.

All of us have moments that we look back on with regret and remorse. Perhaps we spoke thoughtlessly, behaved carelessly, or hurt someone unnecessarily. It can be acutely uncomfortable to remember being a jerk. Our impulse then is to hide from the thoughts, purge the recollection, and stifle the shame. This pattern can easily become a habit. But with an enhanced awareness of self and a goal for happiness, we can learn a new cycle. When a shameful thought arises, we can recall it, accept the emotions it evokes, and then plan future behavior based on new, healthier attitudes. When our thoughts wander, we can ask ourselves: *What do I want to think about next: past, present, or future?* It is a simple yet immensely valuable strategy that puts us squarely on the path toward evolving into someone who learns from mistakes and moves on. It's the best any of us can do, and it is an essential key to happiness.

The same memory of the past is often regarded differently in different states of mind. Developing an awareness of these multiple states enables us to better observe when we are about to transition. What sets you off? When do you overreact? When are you inclined to be too passive? Who pushes your buttons and when? The more you can verbalize questions such as these to yourself and answer them the better you can manage your triggers.

But first, above all, must come a willingness to undertake the work. When you allow disturbing questions to arise and attempt to reach some kind of solid conclusion about them—based on realistic optimism—you are on the path to maturity and to improving the quality of your life as a fully and productively engaged adult in the pursuit of happiness.

In Lesson 9, I'll describe in detail the psychological factors that are needed to survive—and even thrive—in the face of great rage, grief, and sorrow. And I'll demonstrate how, for those with the strength and wisdom of emotional maturity, true happiness can never be totally eclipsed and can be restored in full, in time.

THE VALUE OF GOALS

Aspirations give life focus and purpose, and achieving even the simplest and most ordinary aims has the power to lift a heavy heart. With my patients, I've repeatedly seen how setting and reaching a short-term goal can lead to healing and how designing a long-range vision for the future can lead to a productive and enjoyable life.

During Carol's illness, both the short-term and long-range goals the two of us had for ourselves had been considerably revised, but we did our best to adapt, to set new objectives. She and I discussed remodeling the kitchen. She enjoyed working on the new design. I feared the renovation would be too disruptive. Eventually, reluctantly, she agreed and put the plans aside. Later, I learned she didn't totally give up on the idea. She set the goal for me in a letter she wrote to me before she died—her last thoughts about our life together—that I've reread countless times.

She told me to remodel the kitchen and to find someone new to love. She understood instinctively that a goal, small or large and clearly defined, is halfway to a goal achieved.

To create a life of happiness, you need to know what is important to you. If you're going to have a wonderful life, then your first step must be to figure out what *wonderful* means to you. Sometimes, when I ask new patients what they want, they say, "I don't know," or "I don't care." Then I know that our work together will begin with exploring how to move beyond those responses, to find the passion and excitement that is dormant within them and that will lead them to being "unstuck."

As you approach the exercises and lessons in the chapters that follow, I encourage you to remember your own uniqueness, to trust your desires, to commit to honesty, to be willing to face your painful and negative emotions, embrace your problems, release your expectations, and choose new ways to manage distress. If you are willing to look beyond first solutions and stay in action, I believe you will find your way to personal transformation and achieve an inner harmony that you can never lose and that can never be taken from you.

PART ONE

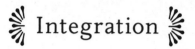 Integration

Finding All the Facets of Self

The first step to becoming all you can be is discovering all that you are, peeling back avoidances to reveal the total and real "I" within.

In our lives, we all play many parts. We are complex, with depths of personality, qualities of character, and a unique, authentic, underlying essence. We can be likened to an onion, with layers that can be peeled back, or to a cut jewel, with many facets that reflect the inner self in different ways at different times. Integration is the result of identifying, acknowledging, and organizing all of the pieces of self and then bringing them together in balance and harmony.

The journey toward integration isn't easy. To some extent, it is the task of a lifetime. We begin as adolescents, struggling to figure out who we are, how we fit in, and what we want from life. We continue to wrestle with these questions as young adults. Most of us imagine that we're going to have it all resolved by our early twenties or at least we think we should. In the 1960s, when hippies popularized the expression *getting your act together,* they were referring to this process of integration. And they recognized it as an ongoing and not-so-easily-reached goal. They pointed out, too, that the older generations certainly couldn't claim to having fully attained it, either.

For emotionally healthy young people, the work of establishing an inner coherence of identity may have progressed quite satisfactorily by the time they completed their education and were ready to step out into the world to begin a career, find a partner, and perhaps start a family. The majority of us would probably say that we encounter many young adults who are solid and full inside. But as therapists know, this is true only up to a point, and it is often mostly in appearance.

Pulling together the sides of the self into an overall sense of organization is a slow, time-consuming process. Many of us don't give it the time it takes. We get busy with life; we want quick solutions; and some of us were raised or have chosen to depend on institutions to tell us how to live. Then later, when we have time on our hands or feel an inner dissatisfaction or are presented with some dilemma or troubling circumstance, we look inside anew and once again take up the work of discovering our many aspects.

As we grow older, we all wish to grow wiser, kinder, and more loving. Self-observation and self-knowledge are the keys to achieving these aspirations. The route to success in this endeavor requires developing skills to look, think, and assess the truths within the heart and mind. One of my most important messages throughout this book is about the process of thinking, specifically how to think about yourself, your goals, and your choices. This is not an easy or automatic achievement, and I will be coming back to it again and again. I want to lead you into the deepest core of your self, to examine all of your mental and emotional processes, conscious and subconscious, not just to soothe a troubled mind but to access the deep, still center of serenity that exists within you. You may live amid turmoil and crises, but all can be well at the center of yourself; your heart can be at peace.

I begin with the premise that you already possess all that you need to achieve dramatic new results in your life. Finding happiness that transcends circumstances doesn't have to mean spending week after week in sessions with a licensed psychiatrist, psychologist, or trained counselor. All that is required is a willingness for deep and honest self-exploration.

Everyone who is evolving and maturing throughout a lifetime can face a need for self-examination to a greater or lesser degree at any time, at any age, no matter how successful, accomplished, or "together" he or she may appear. For example, my colleague Ken was in his mid-forties on the beautiful spring afternoon when I joined him for lunch in our hospital cafeteria and found him grappling with an unwelcome frame of mind. I slid my tray onto the table, took a chair across from him, and said lightly, "Hi, Ken. Nice day, isn't it?" I was looking out at the sun on the eucalyptus forest that flanks one side of our medical campus.

"Maybe for you, but not for me," he growled, looking

down at his food, his expression surly. After a moment, he looked up, smiled wryly, and said, "Sorry, Mardi, I am not myself today."

I am not myself today. That's a familiar, frequently used expression. It's also psychologically interesting and says a great deal when you think about it. Of course, one is always oneself. Ken certainly hadn't turned into another being on that afternoon in May. What he was saying was that the grumpy guy who responded so curmudgeonly to my casual comment was not an aspect of himself that Ken wanted to own. He meant: *I am not my usual, attractive, friendly, upbeat self today*—the self he preferred to present to the world. However, with his smile, he ruefully accepted that he was in a dark mood. He didn't like it, but he had the maturity to know it would pass. Sooner or later, he'd rouse himself from his funk, that place of self-pity.

Like Ken, we all have moods and states of mind that don't measure up to our ideals. Regardless of how we present ourselves to others, in the privacy of our thoughts, we have different selves that emerge in different emotional states. Successful integration requires getting to know this committee of selves, forming a hierarchy, figuring out who is the chairperson of the group, and establishing an overall and long-standing coherent self-organization.

These different self-concepts are formed by a compendium of elements, including the experiences, ideas, values, attitudes, and viewpoints that have come together to make a one-of-a-kind you. Body image, temperament, talents, patterns of interaction, and associated beliefs all contribute to forming self-concepts. And some of these can be in the form of unconscious knowledge, active or inactive in different states of mind, realistic and unrealistic.

Many people have an unrealistic view of their appearance, for instance. They think they are unattractive when others know them to be truly lovely. Some people judge parts of themselves too harshly, or they are grandiose in some ways, inappropriately insecure at others times, or see some of their frames of mind as monstrous or preposterous. Integration isn't handed to us like some well-put-together jigsaw puzzle; it takes work to fit all the pieces together. And irrational or ineffective pieces may need to be revised, completed, or counteracted by rehearsed and rational attitudes.

TRAITS: THE GOOD, THE BAD, AND THE IN-BETWEEN

In different states of mind, you may find yourself operating on different principles. The values and rules by which you judge yourself may shift. When dominated by a certain view, you might be quite restrained. In another frame of mind, you might find a way to justify reckless or flamboyant behavior. Different self-concepts create different states of mind and different emotional colorations.

It is not unusual to possess polar opposite traits: our altruistic side verses our selfish side, our procrastinating self verses our responsible self, our loner self verses our party-animal self, our desire for immediate gratification versus our long-term goals. All of these parts can be harmonized by paying attention to them and their contradictions, consciously deciding what is most important at any specific time, and by practicing moderation, avoiding the extremes. There are no quick solutions to integrating and prioritizing our conflicting parts.

Working on self-integration means acknowledging desired and dreaded parts of one's self and accepting personal complexity. This is a continuing process that must include tolerance for ambiguities and even nastiness. Knowing one's self means acknowledging and accepting a full range of self-appraisals and feelings, including pride and shame, optimism and pessimism, exaggeration and minimization. As well, it's necessary to appreciate realistic goals, roles, and values, even if you may not want to conform to convention.

HAL: A COMMITTEE OF SELVES

A handsome thirty-year-old, Hal had various self-images, from pretentious and unrealistic to shameful and overly humble to level-headed and accurate. He saw himself as a committed husband, an adoring father, a man of means, a rising star in his profession, the owner of a prestigious home, a man attractive to women, the envy of his peers, and the captain of his fate.

In our sessions together, he and I worked to identify all his many aspects. He came to call one part of himself "my vanity." From this frame of mind, he believed all his dreams could come true, nothing could stand in his way, and he could have it all. After all, he was only thirty, and he was already in a middle-management position of authority. He also secretly believed that because he was such a hunk and a great lover, his wife should overlook his occasional brief affairs. And because he was giving his daughter such a great life and secure future, he felt that she shouldn't really miss him not being around much of the time.

On the flip side, Hal called another part of himself "my state of insecurity." When he was in this frame of mind, he worried and excoriated himself. Had he done enough to get the promotion at work? He had a master's degree in business administration, and yet he still earned under $100,000 per year. People would certainly be critical of him for that, wouldn't they? He wondered if his wife might be losing interest in him. Sometimes he felt their child was a much higher priority with her than he was. He also doubted his skills as a father. Other men seemed to understand their kids, whereas he often felt clueless around his daughter. What would happen when she got older? Would he be even worse at parenting?

With these two frames of mind, Hal shifted from exhilaration and an inflated sense of empowerment to anxiety and an exaggerated sense of self-disgust. Neither was realistic or rational.

But Hal had another frame of mind that he called "me, more or less as I really am." When in a mood organized by his realistic self-concepts, he felt a bit of legitimate pride. He was moving along well enough in his life, and he was striving to make it even better, both professionally and personally, in his genuine efforts to improve his relationship with his family and in his work with me. He knew his life could be ruined by an affair. He knew he would have to work long hours to save the large sum he desired. He knew he was not yet the best man he could be.

In our sessions, Hal worked to develop a new self-coherence. By examining all the elements in the matrix of his self-appraisals and conceptualizations, he came to understand how he used fantasy to stimulate himself out of his leaden states of self-disgust. That is, he overrode his dark and uncomfortable frames of mind and stirred excitement within by imagining himself as a stud who could get away with an extramarital affair, or as a corporate hotshot who couldn't be stopped, or as a man of wealth who could have it all. As he became more in touch with his central, realistic self-concept, he faced the reality that he was neither a stud muffin nor an incompetent underachiever. Both those self-images were exaggerated and erroneous—inappropriately grandiose and unnecessarily insecure. Reasoning about this strengthened his realistic beliefs. He learned that, when he found himself falling into a sinkhole of deflated emotion, he could use his sense of core authenticity rather than a fantasy persona to rouse himself from it. With his new self-reflective awareness he was better able to ride out his low periods. He had more tolerance for them. And he gained new skills to alter his dark moods with realistic self-talk rather than with dangerous and self-defeating fantasies.

Hal also worked to sort out his goals, values, and

choices wisely, to revise his agenda. And by coming to know his different self-states and sorting out his rational and irrational beliefs, Hal could chart a course of both action and self-restraint that could lead to the fulfillment of his goals. It was a very hard task, but he found his way to greater integration, a much more realistic self-conceptualization, and a new sense of inner harmony.

BELLA: GETTING REAL ABOUT THE SELF

Another patient with competing—and opposing—self-concepts in need of identifying, reevaluating, and balancing first came to my office because she had been ordered to consult a therapist. Bella was an intelligent, highly competent, thirty-five-year-old computer programmer who had been passed over for a promotion, despite her excellent performance. Deeply angry and resentful, she began showing up at work under the influence of alcohol and continued to drink during her lunch hour. Her behavior didn't go unnoticed, of course. She was soon referred to her corporation's human resources department, where she was told that if she didn't want to lose her job she would have to get counseling and treatment for her drinking.

In her first session with me, Bella made it crystal clear that she was there grudgingly, only because it was mandatory. She was also unequivocal in her feelings about not being promoted. She saw it as an outrageous injustice.

"Even if it was completely unjust, why would you shoot yourself in the foot because of it?" I asked her.

"Showing up at work under the effects of alcohol will only lead to you losing your job and hurt your future. It's no way to get even, is it?"

"It will show them that I can outperform anyone there in any kind of condition," she told me.

"Well, that is clearly a defiant and self-defeating kind of magical thinking," I said. "And it's not doing you any good."

The words *magical thinking* caught her by surprise. I could see that she was insulted by my assertion and still rebellious but also intrigued by the expression. She dropped her guard a little, and we began to talk about her patterns of thought and action.

Since childhood, Bella had had a long record of astonishing intellectual skills. She was intuitive and very fast. She carried out computer programming with amazing speed. She just seemed to know, without even thinking it through, how to solve a difficult problem. She'd simply jump in, follow her instincts, and the solution would appear before her. This was a great skill, and it made her something of a techno-wizard, but it did not work effectively in other areas of her life, which she failed to realize.

The potent Wonder Woman self-image, the ability to pull a rabbit out of a hat was exciting and rewarding for Bella. The thrill of jumping into something without knowing the end result gave her a rush and a kick. It also doomed her to failure when she plunged rapidly ahead into projects before she had all the pieces she needed to finish the job. For example, in the remodeling of her new condominium, she was a capable carpenter, but she had a tendency to cut wood before she'd measured it several times, thus wasting valuable materials. Naturally, she knew better. Yet, when she was in a buoyant, self-confident frame of mind, she'd tell herself, *I can do this, and I can do it right away.*

So why was she allowing herself this excessive self-harming magical thinking, I asked her. What purpose did this exalted state of mind serve? Did it eclipse another side of her that perhaps wasn't thrilling at all but darker and uncomfortable?

After giving it some thought, she admitted that it did. She had an aspect of herself that she called "sourness." When it arose, she felt agitated, despondent, bitter, and incompetent. She felt like an inept child who hated the world. Magical thinking produced thrills that got her out of her sour state.

Another side of Bella also served to blanket the sourness, "the superior critic" who believed she could outperform everyone and who didn't like to have her thoughts or actions questioned. In our sessions, when Bella was in this frame of mind and I would try to direct her attention to something, she'd flare up and snap at me for interfering with her train of thought. She told me that she felt like a preoccupied scientist interrupted by a pea brain. I would say that if she were to behave this way at work, it certainly wouldn't improve her career. Over time such a grandiose and unrealistic point of view would, in fact, annoy her colleagues, lead to conflicts, and ultimately deflate her self-esteem even further.

There was within Bella another state of mind, a more realistic, restrained, and grown-up self-concept. In this calm, reflective mode, Bella was not a superior critic, an insecure little girl, or Wonder Woman. She was able to listen and consider my remarks without feeling insulted, angry, or retaliatory. This latter self-schema was obviously the one she needed to install as the chair of her committee of selves as she tried to understand her self-concepts.

As she began to do more of this work, our therapeutic relationship evolved. She grew more and more to see me not as an adversary or critic who attacked her but as a counselor who was helping her to appreciate her own brilliance and to use it to act in her own best interests. In looking toward the future, it was very important for Bella to get real, to understand her tendency toward grandiose thoughts and impulsive actions. Yes, these states of mind lifted her spirits and made her feel great, but they were sometimes unrealistic and then led to dismal end results. So the challenge was how to get the thrill of creative productivity without this handicap. The answer was thinking better: continuing to trust her brilliance while increasing self-restraint. Understanding this equation gave Bella better control of how she made decisions and the ability to recheck them. She was gradually able to reduce her grandiose thinking while retaining the states in which she felt thrilled by her skills and her intuitive development of new computer programs. The praise she began to receive for her excellent work bolstered her motivation and increased her sense of self-worth.

Bella and I also had to address her outbursts of snide anger. I was not the only pea brain in her world. Bella sniped at most people who crossed her path, including supervisors, subordinates, family, and friends. She always had a pretty fair reason to justify her frustration and irritability, but her responses were clearly more hostile than the circumstances warranted. She had a reservoir of bitterness that, it turned out, was left over from childhood grievances and nursed into adulthood. New understanding and forgiveness—issues I'll be discussing in depth in later chapters—were in order. Suffice it to say, Bella worked on these factors as well, and eventually her hair-trigger outbursts and tendency to transfer old resentments into the present diminished.

By the time we completed our work together, Bella's employers were regularly rewarding her job performance, but her greater achievement was in the increased confidence and contentment she had raised within herself.

IDENTIFYING YOUR SELF-SCHEMAS

There is only one way to discover all the pieces of self: You must set aside time for self-reflection. You can do this in many ways, such as through scheduled appointments with a professional counselor, in conversations with a trusted friend, or totally on your own. Creative-writing classes are a way to explore personal issues, as are mutual help groups and contemplative reading about the lives of others. In a sense, we all have recovery work to do, whether or not we suffer from addictions to substances or behaviors. Divorce, illness, separation, unemployment, bankruptcy, as well as workaholism, codependency, and deaths in families all call forth a need for clarity, balance, and harmony.

There are many devices and tools that can be helpful. Some people benefit from writing in a journal, others from asking questions of themselves while looking in a mirror or sitting across from an empty chair and exploring ideas aloud. There's no need to feel foolish. There is a school of "silent therapy," in which the therapist refrains from responding precisely so the patient may hear the words that he or she has spoken hanging in the air, thereby gaining a fresh perspective. The point is to increase your understanding of yourself through whatever techniques feel and work best for you, even if that means speaking with an imaginary therapist. Growth begins the moment a new insight is gained. An *aha!* moment can happen at any time, whether you are alone, in a counselor's office, or in a discussion group or congregation with dozens of other people.

We all carry around personal "baggage": successes, failures, attachments, losses, obligations, values, relationships, careers, habits, hurtful past episodes, shameful memories, recurring thoughts, churning emotions, and much more. Often our history has such unremitting momentum that we get carried along in the tide and forget about stopping to consider the elements of the inner landscape rushing by.

So consider the committee of voices in your head, the roles you fill, the roles you think you are *supposed* to fill, your qualities of character, and your shortcomings. Play archaeologist in your own life and look for all your buried truths. Play anthropologist and look into the familial and cultural sources of some of your intuitive principles. Make these beliefs more conscious and reflect on how you feel about them now.

You are not looking for multiple personalities; you are searching for the integration of a healthy psyche. And while I want to encourage you to discover all your self-concepts, I want to discourage you from any kind of fragmentation. Therapists sometimes have trouble with the language that is used to explain this idea of the layers of self. We use words such as *facets, pieces, aspects, sides,* and *roles,* but the point to remember is that these form an organized, whole identity that is solid and full, however much it might still be a work in progress.

For most individuals, there are three levels of integration:

- Harmonized
- Conflicted
- Discordant

These are somewhat fuzzy categories that can overlap. I'm using them here only to illustrate how you might identify your current level of integration and where you want to be. The goal for all of us, of course, is to achieve the emotional maturity to weather good and bad times and the ups and downs of life with equanimity and wisdom.

Someone at a harmonized level of integration has a coherent self-organization and is able, most of the time, even when under stress or in a negative mood, to make clear, thoughtful decisions without paralysis, to feel authentically responsible for his or her own choices in a complex world, and to act empathetically, recognizing responsibilities that go beyond the self.

An individual at a conflicted level of integration experiences difficulty in dealing with complex emotional situations. He or she may find some intense feelings too hot to handle, misinterpret the circumstances of the moment because of subtle distortions in thinking, project too much of the past onto the present, and/or repeat cycles of maladaptive relationship patterns. This can be seen in the single woman who chooses the same wrong guy for herself over and over again, or in the guy we've all encountered who always has to know it all and control everything.

A person with discordant sets of self-concepts is one who lives at different times in different frames of mind and who is vulnerable to intense emotional states, meltdowns, and extreme black-and-white attitudes. Because this individual's self-images are not consciously acknowledged, balanced, or connected, he or she can suddenly become erratic, impulsive, cold, hot, grandiose, hostile, or act with extreme self-disgust. People at discordant levels of integration have a tendency to distort reality and are often unable to view others as equals. In changing states, they may exchange one set of distorted reasoning for another or suddenly appraise a situation with total rationality, unaware of their vacillation.

But this doesn't mean that such a person lacks intelligence, charm, or a knack for accomplishing tasks and reaching high leadership positions. Volatile bosses who fly into explosive rages are not at all uncommon, as many of us have discovered. And we've all probably met more than one man or woman who, fueled by self-righteousness and/or indignation, uses others as though they are objects and never accepts responsibility, blaming every failure on someone else.

Sometimes a period of stress, unexpected circumstances, or an important event can illuminate a lack of integration. For instance, someone who is used to being in charge and caring for others, such as a physician, can show his true colors if he is suddenly the patient. If he has accomplished harmonized integration, this switch in roles won't throw him. He'll treat his caretakers with respect, ask for help, and accept it gracefully and appreciatively. But if his integration is conflicted or discordant, tensions will abound—and woe to the people around him! The actor William Hurt played this role eloquently in the movie *The Doctor*. Conflicting attitudes of wanting to ask for help and appearing too needy will lead to shifts from resentment to self-disgust and perhaps explosive rages.

Another example might be a bride on her wedding day who, if she has attained harmonized integration, can be a shining star of loveliness throughout all the pomp and festivities. But if her integration is conflicted or discordant, beware of the emotional fireworks that may get set off if one of her fantasies about the ceremony is thwarted. A cable network has even developed a show, aptly called *Bridezillas,* that illustrates this pattern with crystal clarity.

It can be easy and somewhat smugly satisfying to watch, identify, and judge another person's level of integration, but it's quite a bit more difficult to recognize our own. Before we can move forward, however, we need to acknowledge that all of us are working our way through these levels and that age and accomplishment don't necessarily mean that balance and harmony have been reached. There are plenty of grandparents who still suffer from insecurities, retirees who inappropriately need to show off or are excessively self-absorbed, and senior citizens who've never learned to handle their emotions. For all of us, the work is ongoing, and being truthful about what level you've achieved is important in determining what goal you need to reach.

Exercise: Organizing Your Self-Concepts

Start by relaxing. Staying calm and reflective is key. My patient Bella's progress took off as soon as she realized that my stance with her was not that of a critic but that of a commentator who was simply directing her attention to consider a point and who remained unruffled by her sniping. This is the position I encourage you to take with yourself: not to flinch and turn away when an unpleasant facet of yourself arises but to acknowledge and appraise it. At this point, you are trying to clarify the aspects of yourself and begin the process of revising what does not work. Be willing to stick with the process, although there may be times when you feel shaky about what is happening, unsure if anything is changing.

The work of integration is like the work of a composer, bringing all the parts into harmony.

STEP 1: Give yourself plenty of time. Multiple sessions are better than one appraisal. Take a dose-by-dose approach.

STEP 2: Clarify your ideal self-concepts, your derogatory ones, and the more realistic aggregates of beliefs about who you are.

Make a list of your self-concepts. List making is such a common practice, it's rarely thought of as significant, but a list can be a powerful tool for gaining self-knowledge, a rich source of clarity and growth. A list is private, easy to expand, and can go on and on. It is a summary, an overview, a kind of blueprint that may guide you to the future. Looking down at your list can be like looking down on the whole from a higher plane, allowing you to see the interconnections.

Look to discover the opposites within. Bella and Hal each had relatively positive self-images that helped them deal with the negative self-concepts causing their dark and sour moods. Questioning yourself can help you see through the layers of your inner world.

You might find an ideal self and an unwanted self. You might want to be just like your mother but know you are not. Or you definitely do *not* want to be like your father but, recognize that you are. If you realize that you are sometimes grandiose, consider if that self-concept might exist to compensate for feeling inferior in another state of mind. Both views are extreme and irrational, but, with acknowledgment, you can begin to find your way to moderation. Perhaps you recognize a part of yourself that is very competitive and ambitious. You're eager to get ahead, but there is also a part of you that likes being liked. You want to be popular at work. Your ambitious self may conflict with your sociable self, which can give rise to damned-if-you-do/damned-if-you-don't dilemmas.

STEP 3: Reevaluate each attribute or attitude, looking for erroneous, outmoded, or misapplied beliefs.

Aspects of self develop as we mature, but that doesn't mean old aspects get expunged. In your self-examination you might find that there is still a part of you that maintains your childhood and adolescent views. Ask yourself what messages you received as a kid about how to be: *Be nice. Be strong. Be quiet.* What "don't be" messages were you given? *Don't be a sissy. Don't be a smart aleck. Don't be the center of attention. Don't be like everyone else.* Another means of exploring these depths is to ask yourself what your parents most feared you'd become. *A dropout? A nonchurchgoer? An unemployed freeloader? A corporate robot? A Republi-*

can? A Democrat? A childless career woman? A house-wife and mother with no career or creative interests? How did these messages influence your self-image? Many of the self-concepts that are developed in early life are worth keeping; some are not. It's good to know the difference.

STEP 4: Reassemble the traits that seem realistic.

This exercise provides a kind of central organization from which you can contemplate the interconnections of all your parts. Your opposing views need to be priori-tized or compromised, balanced, and aligned with your goals and values.

STEP 5: Make new choices.

Look for more apropriate attitudes to counteract the beliefs you'd like to change. Arriving at a new under-standing and reorganizing your priorities and values can be a fast road to greater inner peace. New connections will empower you and increase your self-esteem. Focus on the future. Part of the work is imagining yourself in various possible futures, with various possible future selves. The past is worth addressing if you are inappro-priately projecting it into the present; otherwise you are trying to bottle water that has already gone down the drain. Your goal is to use your most realistic self-schema in organizing your thoughts, feelings, and actions, and to keep this realistic self as close to your ideal self as possible. In other words, to rework the extremes to build a reality-grounded sense of a central self.

STEP 6: Practice new actions.

Hal learned to handle his low periods by giving up his fantasies and engaging in new self-talk. Work at developing the new attitudes you arrived at to replace your outmoded or self-defeating views. Old patterns feel normal; altering them involves actions that at first may feel awkward until you repeat them often enough so that they become natural.

STEERING A STEADY COURSE

Have you ever worried that you missed your chance at happiness? Have you wondered if you chose the right college, the right major? Have you made the best career choices for yourself? Did you marry too young? Did you turn down a proposal and now wonder if that was a mistake? Did you fail somehow, somewhere along the line to recognize your golden opportunity when it came knocking?

It's natural to ponder the road not taken, but it's irrational to fear that you've missed some door that opens into a perfect world. There is no perfect world. Yet this idealized concept is firmly planted within the human psyche.

As a young person, you were full of dreams. You anticipated what your life would be like. You envisioned a glorious future. But then, in the day-to-day course of living, you found a discrepancy between what you imagined and your actual experience. You may think: *By now, I should have a good income, creative work, a good relationship, a life without stress.* When you look around and it appears that others have totally wonderful lives, your sense of being stuck or left behind is reinforced. A nagging question arises that asks: *If I'd made different choices, would I now be in a better place?*

This tension, frustration, and dissatisfaction can come when parts of the self are not well linked, when roles and values are out of harmony. To help yourself out of this state of mind, it's essential to realize fully that life is not perfect and then to focus on realistic choices and already existent blessings. No one can have it all. This may seem obvious and simplistic, yet it's a very important and difficult lesson that many of us struggle to learn. It's not easy to give up expecting and wanting all our desires to be met, to stop believing, as we are so often told, that if we work hard enough, are savvy enough, "together" enough, visualize or pray enough, all our wishes will be granted. There's sorrow in admitting that some dreams will never come true. We must mourn for that which can never be, but once the reality of imperfection is accepted and absorbed, the need to fear the absence of some ideal dream is gone. The way is opened for lucid trains of thought and much clearer decision making. There's room for new hope. Life can be happy rather than perfect.

FREDERICKA: ALL GROWN UP WITH TEENAGE DREAMS

This thirty-five-year-old wife and mother was being defeated by a persistent but unconscious adolescent dreaminess. She decided to consult a therapist when she starting experiencing unmanageable and unpredictable irritation at her family, friends, coworkers, and strangers alike. Reviewing and analyzing her situation with me, she painfully admitted that her life wasn't going in the direction she wanted.

Although her marriage was stable and satisfying and she had a two-year-old daughter she adored, Fredericka felt unhappy, steeped in a sense of stagnation. In the last five years she'd made a series of unsatisfying personal and career compromises. She had a passion for drawing and wanted to exhibit and sell original work, but she found the profit-driven art establishment alienating and hostile. To be financially successful, she believed she'd have to abandon her artistic vision for the sake of commercial viability. She was employed as an architectural technician, drafting and coloring three-dimensional plans, an occupation that she found stifling. She also hated leaving her little girl in daycare, but that was a necessity; her household needed two incomes. She and her husband frequently fantasized about traveling together, and she wanted another child despite knowing that a larger family would mean even less time and money for everything else she wanted to do.

Focusing on this predicament made her angry and frustrated. Fredericka had many values she did not want to compromise and many roles she wanted to fill—wife, mother, artist, world traveler, breadwinner, home owner, community contributor—all wonderful, all worthwhile, and all overwhelming since they were not prioritized, balanced, or harmonized.

In her therapy sessions, she came to recognize how she'd been operating on the principle that she *should* be able to have it all. She realized that she needed to make compromises, accept some limitations in her life, and readjust her expectations. When she accepted this reality, her situation bloomed with possibilities. If she could not have a perfect world, there was no need to fear she was missing out on it. She began to reprioritize her agenda. Given the reality of her biological clock, a second child was a more important immediate goal, she decided, than the pursuit of her artistic career. The big house could wait and so, too, the extensive travel. For now, she could look for work as an illustrator, which would give her more artistic freedom than drafting. She might also set aside a few hours a week for uninterrupted studio time so that she could draw. Later, when both children were in school, she could pursue a master's degree in fine art and perhaps seek a teaching position that might give her even more studio time. This mature thinking enabled her to increase her self-governance, which, in turn, decreased her irritability. Rather than turning from one task to the next in explosive shifts and never feeling that anything had been completed satisfactorily, her revised attitude made her more content. In fact, she was more fulfilled in every role once she had thoroughly considered all the aspects of herself and allocated an appropriate amount of time for each of them. She bartered with another mother to have some well-defined hours to herself. Being a mother and being an artist no longer competed. She found creative self-expression in both roles. And by discussing and negotiating more with her husband, her marriage grew stronger. Yes, she had compromised, but she felt in greater control, having achieved a vital balance. She was living a life full of blessings and future promise.

During our work together, while she was in the midst of her conflict, Fredericka felt less integrated and more chaotic in the sense of who she was. But in the long run, once she'd worked through her problems, the process provided her with a more coherent identity and greater self-confidence and pride.

For all of us, clarifying some dilemma and then making and implementing new positive choices leads to integration, and it feels great to grow. On the other hand, it feels lousy to be stuck. Our prickliest conflicts aren't those between good and evil; black-and-white decisions are easy to make. It's the gray area that causes us trouble, the quandaries that present us with contradictory motives, neither of which is necessarily good or bad.

SUSAN: EMBRACING AMBIVALENCE

A twenty-six-year-old, midlevel manager at a public relations firm, Susan became overwhelmed and indecisive when she thought about competing for a promotion in her department. She wanted the prestige, salary, and opportunities of the senior position, but she didn't want to be seen as too aggressive or jeopardize the warm relationship she had with her colleagues. Her coworker Carl had made it clear that he was hungry for the advancement and that he didn't want anyone in his way. He obviously expected her to back off.

Susan might have explained to him that she was also interested in the position. She could have suggested an agreement that they each would make a best case for the spot, accept the decision of their supervisors with good grace, and maintain a positive regard for each other. But she was too paralyzed with anxiety, too afraid of a possible angry confrontation, too reluctant to risk the stability of her work environment. In the end, she did nothing. Carl got the promotion, and Susan felt miserable. It wasn't the first time she'd become frozen in a competitive/cooperative situation. It was a pattern, but now she was frustrated and disgusted enough with herself to consult a therapist to see if she couldn't find her way out of such self-sabotage.

Susan began to identify and correct her maladaptive pattern. She had a therapist to guide her, but anyone trying to overcome similar repeating self-defeating responses and behaviors can follow the same steps.

First, she focused on identifying the repetitive cycles, letting go of self-disgust, putting aside self-judgment, and looking squarely at the facts. It was obvious Susan had difficulty dealing with conflicting priorities. When she was ambivalent about a situation, she would switch back and forth between reasons for taking an action and reasons for not acting.

This style of vacillation was also evident in her relationship with her boyfriend, Felix. She admired and enjoyed him in some ways and found him lacking in others. He made less money than she did and had fewer career ambitions, which frustrated her, although she wondered if she was being unfair in her expectations of him. She ordered him about because she wanted things done. He didn't object to taking her direction, which made him seem passive and weak to her. Yet she felt bad that she took advantage of his good nature.

Disdainful of him, she broke off the relationship. Later, yearning intensely for his company, she called him, apologized, and asked to resume where they'd left off. Felix, angry and distant, refused. Susan was surprised as well as unsettled and confused by his huffiness. Part of her was desperate to get back together with him; part of her was relieved the relationship might really be over. Her conflicting feelings left her torn, in acute discomfort, full of self-doubt and anxiety—a direct result of her lack of clarity about her goals, roles, intentions, values, and priorities. Susan had not connected the diverse elements of her personality.

She wanted to be in charge—in her relationships and in her work environment—but she held back from full throttle. At work, she would start an action that she thought would impress her supervisors but then stop short of fully demonstrating her competence and productivity. She had anxiety that winning a competition meant hurting a coworker. She also did not want to feel humiliated that her very best work was not good enough. Being in the driver's seat in a relationship meant defeating and humiliating her partner. Letting someone else be in charge meant that she was weak and being manipulated.

This distorted thinking carried into her therapy, where she wanted to be told what to do and advised on how to cope to avoid her own self-criticisms. Yet she resented advice or clarifications of her pattern of behavior because receiving these suggestions made her ashamed of her own passivity.

Eventually Susan came to see the inappropriateness of these attitudes and to use her intelligence and reasoning to revise her beliefs. She recognized these irrational views came from her past. Her father had dominated and ordered her mother about. To Susan, his role seemed preferable; he was clearly stronger. Yet she did not like her father's attributes, and she loved her mother. It took time for Susan to become conscious of her trains of thought, acknowledge, and then redirect them. It didn't occur at warp speed, but she came to understand that developing and emphasizing new, more situationally appropriate attitudes could counteract the old distorted beliefs.

Before getting her various self-roles together, Susan could not make and then stick with a difficult decision. She either acted impulsively to escape the pain of confusion, such as breaking up with Felix, or she became paralyzed and didn't act at all. Susan could not consciously decide whether to dominate another person, cooperate, or subordinate herself. As a result, ambivalence and vacillation as well as oscillation between the extremes prevented her from developing her competence and confidence.

Susan engaged in unconscious either/or thinking. In therapy, when she put her thought process into words and observed the patterns, she gained insight into her attitudes and established a framework for recognizing when her thinking fell into extreme polarities in the future. For example, in her situation with Felix, several lines of inner dialogue caught her by surprise when she finally uncovered them.

1. *If I break up with him, I'll be hurting him unnecessarily and that will make me feel guilty, as if I did something bad. So to avoid feeling guilty, I will stay with him.*
2. *If I leave him, I will be lonely. Since I'm unlovable, I won't be able to get anyone better. So I will hold on to our relationship because it's the best I can get.*
3. *If I stay with him, I'll feel trapped. I am the stronger person; I'll dominate him. He'll feel bad, and I'll feel more guilt. Anyway, he is too weak for me. Breaking up with him is the only way to escape the kind of bad relationship my parents had.*

By stating her premises so clearly, Susan could consciously work on her attitudes and revise them. She could find many other ways out of her otherwise life-stagnating dilemmas. She could reconsider all her parts, altering unrealistic expectations and false conclusions, such as the belief that she is unlovable (which is how her mother regarded her), or that she must be unlike her mother in order to be lovable.

For all of us who are struggling to harmonize and balance all the pieces of self, reappraisals can bring old and new pieces together in a new way. Our dilemmas might still exist, but with more realistic ideas and manageable emotions, we can make better decisions.

Teaching Points

- Your self-esteem, your skill at coping with adversity, and your ability to pursue happiness all depend in part on how well you integrate conflicting beliefs and values. This process begins by acknowledging the many aspects of yourself, including your best and worst attributes.
- You must also clearly analyze your rational and irrational beliefs about yourself. Learning to tolerate some negative feelings, even momentary self-disgust, is essential to the process.
- Look for your self-defeating behaviors. Ask yourself what could have triggered them. Do they protect you in some way? Do they help you to avoid other uncomfortable states of mind? Undesirable conduct usually has a reason behind it. Once you've found it, you can deal with it in a new way.
- What causes you to overreact? If you can identify what pushes your buttons, you can begin disconnecting them by developing more mature and rational responses to your triggers.

- Examine your past carefully. Identify decisions and actions that you regret. What would you do differently if the same circumstances reoccurred? Practice the new attitudes until you begin to feel comfortable with them.
- Are there opportunities that you did not pursue and still think about longingly? Are there times when you experience jealousy because someone has something you do not? Often jealousy can turn into self-judgment: You put yourself down for failing to acquire what others have. Let these unpleasant emotions help you identify what is missing from your life. Consider them a reminder that you have a goal. Happiness doesn't require having every desire fulfilled. We can be perfectly satisfied while working to achieve our aims.
- Think about your long-range future. Set goals that will foster your happiness in the years to come rather than simply indulge in immediate gratification or relieve present tension or a current conflict.
- Prioritize your dreams, and determine whether your goals are compatible rather than mutually exclusive. Be aware that you may need to make compromises in order to take a realistic and step-by-step approach to achieving what is truly important to you. You also may have to act boldly without having every fact available. At all costs, avoid ending your train of thought on catastrophic possibilities of any choice and thoughts such as *Who am I kidding? I'll never be able to do this!* This kind of

thinking simply destroys dreams. Remember you won't get everything that you want; no one does. And when you do fulfill a desire, it may not be in quite the way you expected. You don't have control of the universe, but you do get to create your own vision of heaven on earth and then celebrate the results.

- Don't forget the process is ongoing, the work of a lifetime. Never give up, and keep advancing your efforts at integration throughout your life.

The Importance of
Self-Reflection

*The second step to building internal peaceful-
ness and establishing harmonized integration is
to develop thinking skills that will allow you to
clarify emotional conflicts and establish personal goals.*

When a patient enters therapy, their doctor, analyst,
or counselor leads the way. But the process can be
embarked on alone by anyone who is willing to engage
in an honest examination of his or her inner landscape.
In this chapter and the ones that follow, I'll be walking
you step-by-step through a series of lessons that will lead
to greater self-awareness and understanding, showing
you how to focus on one issue at time and helping you
to recognize your expectations, set realistic goals, and
overcome troubling memories and other frustrating difficulties that may block your progress. Your aim will be
to think freely, to let your thoughts come willy-nilly, but

also, paradoxically, to direct your thinking, to dig for the ideas and feelings that are deeply buried, and to leave no thought "unthought."

To begin, you need to prepare yourself for the journey. Your first requirement is to be in the right frame of mind. Ideally, this is a state of calm contemplation, in which you are poised to set aside time, sit down, and give your undivided attention to an emotional topic, while holding at bay any intense feelings, such as rage, fear, guilt, shame, and/or sadness. Professional psychotherapists call this state a "mental set." Arriving at this state is like getting in your car and turning the dials on the thermostat to the right temperature and airflow before you begin your trip. You establish your intent and ready yourself to think about a chosen subject while remaining fully aware of your feelings, without allowing them to distract or overwhelm you.

Don't expect clear sailing in trying to be lucid about difficult issues in your life. You are sure to be buffeted by winds of powerful emotions. You may often feel stuck. And don't expect insights and enlightenment to come swiftly. Serious self-examination is like painting a complex portrait. It involves many layers of color and a subtle blending of tones, light, and shadow before a rich, full, multifaceted picture emerges. Throughout this book, I'll be suggesting ideas and giving you tools to help you peel away the layers and break through barriers.

While you're looking at all the components of your unique personality and life experience, you are almost certain to encounter traits that distress you. No one is perfect. We all have weaknesses and darkness within. You may not like what you see. But awareness of your undesirable traits is important. This knowledge can motivate you to change. And it is through examining the thinking behind the characteristics and behaviors you most dislike in yourself that you will find your way to a new and better you.

When I began my residency in psychiatry, I was often shocked by what I saw, the range of distress, delusions, illusions, and hallucinations. I had no idea that people could be so extreme. In time, I got over my stunned reaction. But as I gained the knowledge and skills I needed to treat and help patients, I received the support of the experienced faculty members who worked with me. They encouraged me to look at the amazing properties of the human mind with a sense of wonder. Now, in my turn, I want to pass along this point of view.

In self-contemplation, an attitude of wonderment rather than self-disdain can help you to be kinder to yourself and to feel much more comfortable when you open up. A sense of awe can replace, or at least ameliorate, severe self-criticism. With this perspective, you can stay aware longer and be less likely to shut down under the stress that a passage of change may require.

So as you proceed on this adventure of self-discovery, I encourage you to give up the self-talk that says *How could I have been so stupid!* And, instead, say to yourself *Would you look at that! Isn't it amazing that I could believe and feel that way?*

I also encourage you to greet new ideas with friendly

curiosity. Test every idea. Air all your intuitions. Brainstorm. Follow your hunches. Remember that even the most outrageous and "dangerous" idea might contain the seed of something that could be useful to you. Above all, avoid a doom-and-gloom mentality. Remaining realistic is not the same as subscribing to pessimism. Optimism and courage bolster self-confidence and motivate you to forge ahead. These qualities are not investments from cosmic forces or gifts bestowed on only a lucky few; they are virtues that can realistically be cultivated by anyone who wants to possess them and who is willing to do the work.

BEGINNING YOUR LINE OF QUESTIONING

If you have picked up this book and are reading it, chances are you are someone who is already familiar with introspection and have a strong interest in developing yourself as a human being. When you think about what you want out of life, your choices will fall into three categories:

- What you have: your material wealth
- What you do: your range of talent, skills, or activities
- What you are: the development of your soul and spirit

All three are important, although many people devote themselves only to the first two categories. They spend all their time and energy defining themselves by their circumstances, by what they *have*—be it money, real estate, clothes, cars, relationships, degrees, or trophies—or by their actions, by what they *do* well—be it performing a job, raising children, participating in a competition, or being active in a church, club, or organization. Of course, living requires *having* and *doing* things, but *A Course in Happiness* suggests that you also devote considerable attention to that aspect of your life that goes beyond doing and having.

As you consider topics for self-contemplation, you may want to address certain attainable goals (things to have or do), but much of your effort needs to be directed toward reflecting on your passion, purpose, and values— the more fundamental choices about who you are and who you want to be. You must balance your wants in the realm of circumstances and the realm of action with your growth in the realm of your soul.

When deciding on a topic to contemplate, ask yourself what's on your mind? Do you have anything to get off your chest? Is there some issue you've been avoiding? Perhaps you think that it isn't urgent and that you don't have time to give it attention, but obviously you have to address important issues at some time, whether you want to or not or however you rank them in urgency. If you bury them, they will inevitably emerge later, either as intrusive thoughts, unbidden images, or even bad dreams. Yet too big a dose of the difficult stuff you have roiling within may not allow you to continue to think calmly. This is a psychological reality, and it's important to acknowledge it and approach your inner work with a dose-by-dose plan.

It's okay to table some topics temporarily. It is also okay to decide there are some topics too toxic for you to ever deal with. If there is some aspect of yourself you're not ready to examine because it is too difficult or troublesome to face head on, that's fine for right now, but at least name it and fully acknowledge the discomfort. Tell yourself the truth about what you are not ready to confront, and put it aside for later. Then pick a topic that is less formidable. By the way, naming topics you want to distract yourself from increases your control of your attention. The name of the topic lets you say "here it is coming up again," which you can counteract with your intention to suppress it.

When you are choosing a topic, try to be specific instead of examining something general, such as "I'm unhappy." You could look at how you find your work unfulfilling, or your social life too limited, or your dependence on TV too great.

Remember to see self-evaluation as a means of solving problems and taking charge of your life, gaining new skills, altering behavior, and expanding your happiness. And don't forget that it's just as important to look at your strengths as well as your weaknesses.

There is no contradiction between loving yourself dearly, treating yourself well, and working very hard to change. You can discover this for yourself by doing the exercises that follow. You've been thinking all your life, of course, but how much have you watched yourself doing it? Probably not a lot. Considering the flow of thoughts through our mind doesn't come naturally for most of us, but it's a habit well worth developing. As with any new skill, it requires a lot of effort at first to learn the technique, followed by repetition and practice—mental sweat—to gain proficiency.

Exercise 1: Thinking About Yourself and Your Choices

STEP 1: Get Ready

When you have time to contemplate the topic you've selected, place yourself in a calm frame of mind, and proceed slowly, free from distractions.

Remind yourself:

- To think "clear and fresh," without self-criticism.
- All thoughts and feelings are welcome, and whatever arises will not distract or overwhelm you.
- You will be looking at short- and long-term scenarios, possible consequences from the sublime to the catastrophic, daydreaming and brainstorming. Nothing is off limits. Nothing has to occupy the center of attention all the time.
- To refrain from insisting on problem solving. It may take several attempts before you reach any kind of resolution. Plan to "not be too sure" about your conclusions.

STEP 2: Set the Course

You aren't likely to reach a destination on a road trip if you don't have an idea of which route to take. For a journey into yourself, you also need a general map to guide you. For example, someone considering whether or not to become engaged would want to cover the pros and cons of the three possible choices: to marry, to break off, or to postpone. Someone deciding whether or not to stay with a dull, secure job or quit to take on a riskier, more exciting project would want to consider "What if…" questions, from the most ideal to the most catastrophic to the most likely, realistic outcome in the short and the long run.

STEP 3: Establish Your Perspective

Imagine an inner observer with a bird's-eye view looking down on your thoughts and responses while remaining detached. This viewer will watch the flow of ideas and emotions through your mind and body, identify patterns, and pose questions about:

- Your physical state: Are you tense, relaxed, anxious, antsy, wired, or squirming with discomfort? Do you have butterflies in your stomach, a furrowed brow, a racing pulse, a clenched fist, or a choked-up chest and throat?
- Your mental state: Are you being fanciful, wistful, fatalistic, or overly optimistic or pessimistic? Your goal is to return, gently yet firmly, to realistic thinking.

• Your self-concept: Are you approaching this topic as an adult or are you operating with all the immature resentments and distortions of your child-mind? Do you see yourself as too old to tackle anything risky? Do you think you're so great you deserve special circumstances and extraordinary consequences? Do you see yourself as so weak and inferior that you are not entitled to good things? The answer lies within you. When your observer asks, listen for your true response.

STEP 4: Know When to Conclude

Good thinking about thinking also involves being aware of how big a dose is good for you at any one time. Be alert; it is easy to short-circuit your own efforts by quitting early just to escape the anxiety and discomfort of the experience. But it can be time to stop without reaching a conclusion if you've looked at the full range of your choices, considered your physical and mental states and your self-concept, and noted all the ideas and feelings that arose throughout the session. You can return to the subject later, and your subconscious is likely to be working on the issue even when your conscious mind is no longer occupied with it. This is hard work, and you can—and should—be proud. Always celebrate the difficult and potentially fruitful effort you've made.

NOTE: Are you feeling anxious already, even at this much of a suggestion that you look at a troubling area in your life? Is your heart sinking? Are you depressed or filled with a sense of hopelessness?

If you are you having thoughts such as: *I'll never be able to do this. I won't get it. It won't help. I've been thinking about this problem forever. Nothing will solve it. It's hopeless.* Then you must first work at finding some way to soothe yourself enough to be able to approach the exercise. Set a time limit for thinking that doesn't overwhelm you—say, three minutes—and for that length of time, suspend your certainty that you will fail and shut off your inner critic. You can handle three minutes of anything! And who knows what you may discover? Then you can turn your attention to anything else, while congratulating yourself for those three minutes you spent working on your emotional growth.

FACING THE FUTURE

Perhaps, to you, setting a goal means drawing up a to-do list for the next week or so and then attempting to handle your time well enough to tick off all the items. Or your idea of long-range planning extends no further than organizing a wedding, family reunion, or vacation in advance, and getting ready for those events has left you absolutely overwhelmed and exhausted.

When I mention long-range planning to my patients, I'm not surprised when they react with startled alarm. "I don't have the time or energy to get everything done day-by-day" is a response I hear frequently. "How can I even begin to think about a plan for the next five years?" I'm asked.

Often, the real issue behind this disinclination to make long-range life plans isn't one of time restraints or a level of vigor; it's unconscious anxiety supplemented by immaturity. The immaturity is in expecting that adult life can meet all idealized adolescent goals. Personal creativity, friendship, marriage, parenting, and career satisfaction are like education, politics, and religion: imperfect. Maturity is living with both hope and the recognition of limits. The anxiety comes from the intuitive knowledge that many goals are embedded in damned-if-you-do and damned-if-you-don't dilemmas. How do you grasp both horns while developing maturity? Well, those are topics for the rest of this course.

For the time being, it is difficult but not impossible to consider the rest of your life and to name and claim your deepest hopes, dreams, and ambitions. Looking at your goals means facing the possibility that your heart's greatest wish may be a futile desire. The future can't be predicted. There's no way to know if the plans you make will actually lead you to your goal, and, once you've established what you want, you may imagine that you will then be living with uncertainty and a deep, aching unrequited longing for a long time.

The task of considering your goals and the methods of achieving them will also require you to face your shortcomings. It's difficult to admit weakness, and there's a natural tendency in all of us to choose the less difficult option. Some people go to extraordinary lengths to hide the truth, whether the matter is illegal, immoral, or simply embarrassing. Someone who is drinking three pints of vodka a day, for example, will probably hide that fact—even from him- or herself. Someone who has maxed out her credit cards to support a shopping addiction and is now avoiding calls from credit collectors will most likely try to keep that fact under wraps, as will cheating spouses, embezzling employees, overeaters, and the untidy and disorganized.

In the short term, denial is easier than confronting hard realities. In the long term, denial can be extremely exhausting, limiting the possibility of change and ultimately cheating you out of happiness. But the hard work of honesty and self-examination is worth the effort. When you are truthful about which areas of your life are working well and which are not, you are poised to grow. On the other hand, if you're out of touch with the truth, you can be blind to pressing problems and come up with silly, ineffectual solutions.

Anyone who is familiar with a twelve-step program will recognize how change for addicts in recovery begins with admitting the truth. Step 1 is: *We admit we are powerless over* [whatever] *and that our lives have become unmanageable.* In the same way, a doctor would never begin treatment without first examining and assessing a patient's health, and a fitness trainer would never begin a training program without thoroughly evaluating an exerciser's capabilities. In the same way any psychological therapy must begin with learning what someone is thinking, doing, and feeling.

Straight talk begins the process by unleashing the forces of positive change. Candidness is of primary importance when setting goals. The trick is to have the goal "just right." If your aim is too high, you've set an impossible goal, and yearning for it will only be a source of frustration and anguish. On the other hand, if your aim is too low, you're really not asking yourself to achieve anything new, and you may find your life repetitious and boring. If you are not stretching your mind, skills, and capabilities enough to grow, then you could be missing out on the sense of excitement that's a part of the process of striving.

"Follow your bliss," "live your dream"—these have been catchphrases in recent years, and although I fully support anyone pursuing his or her fantasy, I'm also a firm believer in the necessity of "keeping it real." It's important to take a hard look at your ambitions in light of your ability to pursue them with a chance of success and to remember that you may first need to acquire new skills and test them in safe circumstances before you can experience the exhilaration of fully enjoying your achievement. If you are too optimistic, you may assume that you can accomplish an unclear and intuitive goal with ease, perhaps with the assistance of a higher power or fate. And if you're too pessimistic, you run the risk of holding yourself back, never breaking out to go for the exciting good challenge and the real possibility of victory.

Honest contemplation is the step that can't be skipped. To live your dreams, you must use your reason to view your future through a clear lens, to free yourself from the overstimulation of excessive optimism or from excessive pessimism that can lead to hopelessness and premature defeat.

The lesson here is to align your goals with your skills and opportunities. It's good to think big; it's not good to think *too* big. It's good to take some chances; it's not good to court a catastrophic end to your opportunities for success by taking excessive risks.

Considering the future also means acknowledging that one day you will die. For each of us, the future is finite, and how much time we have left on earth is unknown. Accepting this reality doesn't mean you must dwell on it, nor do you have to ponder and solve metaphysical mysteries about what happens after death, unless that's your inclination.

Many people worry about dying when they are quite young and unlikely to do so. Others worry when they get a serious illness. In later chapters, I will explore the stress that fantasy- and/or reality-based life crises can cause. For now, the point is simply to be open to the truth. Accepting your own mortality will enable you to plan for it in practical ways that will benefit your family and in emotional ways that will benefit both you and them. You can consider your legacy: what you would like to see happen during your entire lifetime. This can be a very emotional and life-changing exercise. Ask yourself: Where do you want to be in the future? Who do you want to be with? Who do you want to be? How would you like to be remembered? What would you most want to accomplish before you die?

What would you most regret *not* doing? The insights, discoveries, and lessons that emerge from your answers may surprise you, but with the clarity you gain you can begin to bring your dreams into sharp focus.

GETTING FREE OF THE PAST

Another reason that my patients may resist setting long-range goals is the common tendency to project the past onto the future. We can all harbor an unconscious expectation that what has happened in our history—especially the bad things—somehow predicts what will happen in the time that lies ahead. We believe that whatever forces have shaped our lives will continue, but this crouching tiger of fear is often a figment of the imagination, and the nameless dread it engenders can be tamed simply by being aware of the shadows of the past that we project, erroneously, onto our expectations of the future.

There is often no good reason why the beliefs derived in your past have to determine or limit what you can do in the future. In fact, if you've experienced trauma, dealt with it, and overcome it, you are all the stronger for the battle, better able than ever to re-create your life from a clean slate. However, if you haven't fully dealt with the past, it can snare you in myriad ways. A legacy of dysfunction that hasn't been acknowledged or unresolved memories can be formidable obstacles to personal growth. But, then again, the simple light of awareness may be all that is necessary to burst through the roadblock.

Attitudes about the past can morph into unconscious aspects of personality or character, or behavioral traits that arise routinely in all or many states of mind. Directive thinking calls attention to such traits or attitudes and can open areas of awareness that were previously hidden. It's almost impossible to change aspects of our lives that hide in shadows, but when we illuminate our flaws, we begin to weaken their power.

BELINDA: SEEING WHAT'S HIDING IN PLAIN SIGHT

My patient Belinda, a forty-five-year-old office manager, had a personal revelation and breakthrough when she took a careful look at something that was so much a part of her, so familiar, she'd never given it a moment of thought in all of her adult life: her posture. Belinda was tall and thin and walked with a long, heavy, and very purposeful stride. She moved with the speed and steadiness of a fast ocean liner slicing through the waves, her upper body angled slightly forward, her shoulders hunched over a bit, and also with a little tightness in the muscles around her mouth.

"My coworkers say they always know when it's me coming down the hall," Belinda told me. "My footsteps make a distinctive *clip-clip* sound."

Thinking about her stance and walk for the first time, she tried to put into words what it reflected about her: "I'm a no-nonsense person," she said. "I get things done. I do whatever is necessary and then move on to the next task."

Belinda was very responsible and capable. She worked hard but joylessly and without a sense of pleasant rhythm or easy flow. Her posture expressed her purposeful inner attitude. When she relaxed the muscles in her shoulders and around her mouth to see how it would feel, it made her uncomfortable. "It seems too loose," she said. When she tensed the muscles again, she noted that her mouth felt "irritated."

Belinda left my office, but she continued her self-monitoring. She practiced tensing and relaxing her muscles, going in and out of the posture that had always been so natural for her, paying attention to how she felt with each change. She was doing consciously for the first time what she had always done reflexively. After several days, to her surprise, when she was in her usual tense posture and noting it, words came into her mind. *I'll show them*, she heard herself thinking.

She was startled as well as puzzled. Who was *I*? Who were *them*? What were *they* being *shown*?

With reflection, the answers came to her. "Well, '*I*' is me, of course," Belinda told me in our next session, "the girl I once was who had to grow up too fast because my mother was such a ninny. '*Them*' are the people who are like my mother, who don't get things accomplished, who are incompetent, neglectful, self-centered. And what I'm showing them is that I can do things and do them well and that through my competence, I'm humiliating them."

Belinda also recognized the element of irritation within herself, the underlying anger, frustration, and judgment. "A part of me is thinking that because *they* didn't get the work done, I have to. Why do I always have to do everything? They *should* have done more."

It had been a long time since Belinda was a child living at home, experiencing the stress of being an adolescent with an imperfect mother, but she'd continued to relate to the world from that former experience. Now, newly aware, she could work to get things done simply because she chose to. She began to focus on her own pride of accomplishment without the need to humiliate "them," who now were nowhere to be found anyway. She relaxed her rigid posture, her demeanor softened. Now much less tense in her work, she felt better—as did her staff. Most important, Belinda had new feelings of pleasure and satisfaction in her personal growth.

ADELE: AVOIDANCE

It's not at all unusual for people who have been hurt or traumatized to duck from distressing memories. It's another obstacle to personal growth, but once you open up to the truth, you can take a step past it and begin to make effective, enduring changes in your life.

When my patient Adele began therapy with me, she was especially reluctant to talk about her childhood and adolescence. "My real life began the day I went away to college," she told me firmly. "When I moved out of my parents' house, I put everything that had happened there behind me and started over with a clean slate."

It would be a neat trick if we could erase the past and

begin again in a "new and improved" version of ourselves any time we wanted. But life doesn't work that way. When we say "My life starts here," we're denying the reality that all of the drama and trauma of our history remains with us. It's a fantasy that the past doesn't have to be reckoned with. In my work, I routinely see how unresolved childhood wounds and disappointments can undermine happiness.

Adele, of course, had good reasons for resisting remembering her early years. Her memories were painful. Her parents argued frequently. On occasion, their fights escalated into violence. When Adele was six, she witnessed a confrontation between them that ended with her father shoving her mother against the stove. The impact caused a pot of boiling spaghetti to spill, physically scarring Adele's mother—and emotionally scarring Adele.

Adele interpreted this violent act as a bright first-grader would: *If you get angry, you go bonkers, and very bad things happen.* So she resolved: *I will never get angry.* To her child's mind, this reasoning made perfect sense. It was a highly effective plan that provided her with a way to protect herself from future violence.

Thirty years later, however, a plan to "never get angry" looks very different. Since Adele had refused to recall her experiences and reconsider her conclusion with a mature adult mind, she put the lid on anger for life. It became a rigid trait. She was overly submissive and withdrawn, a meek thirty-six-year-old woman who blocked any thoughts or ideas that might provoke anger.

Because she was willing to work on integrating all the pieces of her life story, she soon shifted her belief that "anger is always bad" to "anger can be good or bad depending on the circumstances and on how it is expressed." This liberating new conclusion enabled her to reveal her feelings more openly and to live her life with greater authenticity. It brought her new pride, confidence, and greater peace of mind and heart.

I'll return to the obstacles of projecting the past onto the future, failing to recognize entrenched rigid behaviors, and avoiding unresolved memories. Now I want to alert you to the possibility that you may be experiencing unnecessary fears about the future without even quite realizing it. But, like a virus within your hard drive, once you recognize it is there, you can free yourself of it and nurture the courage and stamina you need to progress. And the more skilled you become at navigating the tumultuous waters within, the less out of control you will feel about the unknown future and the more real control you'll gain over what might happen.

DIRECTED THINKING AND GETTING
TO KNOW YOURSELF

If you were to ask two people what they wanted out of life and one said, "I just don't want to be struggling," and another said, "I'd like to retire in twenty years, financially secure and free to devote my time to taking a therapy dog to the nursing home and helping chronically ill and elderly patients," who do you imagine would be most likely to achieve his or her goal?

Right now, you can begin moving closer to achieving your ambitions by creating a clear vision for the future.

For the time being, put aside the question of how you might realize your dreams and simply look at the specifics of what you want. There is power in details, and there will be time enough later to deal with how you might bring your dream to fruition. Now your goal is to explore what you want and to begin to see how your thinking may be helping or hindering you.

Directed thinking requires the same calm state of mind as previously described. As long as you know you are in such a working state, you can ask yourself certain questions and see what answers may pop up. Exercise 2 below, "What Do You Expect?," is designed to help you sort out your goals and clarify your expectations. Remember to be open to whatever arises: You are actually looking for irrational beliefs you can correct. You may be very surprised by the irrational thoughts and beliefs that may unveil themselves—they are often suppressed.

Focusing your thinking this way is the first step to grounding yourself and to aligning what you want with what you believe and thereby greatly increasing your chances for expanding your sense of inner harmony and creating a truly wonderful life.

Exercise 2: What Do You Expect?

It's natural to have expectations about almost every new situation you're about to enter. Sometimes these expectations are realistic. Sometimes they're wishful

---

thinking. Sometimes they're hidden within your own mind. You may have an intuitive sense of what might happen, experience vague emotions, and fleeting images that are like daydreams, but you may not be able to articulate what you are really anticipating. And if you can't consciously name your expectation, you certainly won't be able to examine all the consequences of what might occur with the different choices available to you.

A simple sequence of questions and answers may help you uncover your agenda, assumptions, and just how optimistic or pessimistic you might be.

For any situation you're considering entering or are about to face, ask yourself:

If _____, then _____.

One example of a realistic response might be: *If I go to dental school, then I will become a successful dentist.*

This may not be as easy as it looks. People differ a great deal in how well they are able to articulate their assumptions. You may struggle and need to keep trying before you develop the knack for arriving at an honest answer. Avoid editing yourself if you can. Let your truthful response arise.

Someone who is overly optimistic might really be fantasizing: *If I go to dental school, then I'll have rich and famous patients and I'll marry a hot rock star.*

Someone with a pessimistic perspective might

think: *If I go to dental school, then I'll probably barely pass, and I'll wind up hating my profession.*

At different times and in different frames of mind, you might find that you have all three types of assumptions: ideal outcomes, poor results, and realistic possibilities. There's nothing wrong with that, but you need to be aware of this likelihood so that you'll be able to sort out the realistic from the ridiculous.

Once you're satisfied with your response, move on to the reasons why an action might lead to what you expect. This is the turn on the road map that leads you to: ... because _____.

For example: *If I go to dental school, then I'll succeed without much effort because I'm the son of a successful dentist and it is my right by blood.*

This step in the exercise is important; it exposes any irrational ideas you may be harboring, such as that genetics confers on you some kind of entitlement. It takes effort to probe within yourself and emotional courage to listen to what you may not like to hear. The more deeply rooted the assumption the more difficult it will be to uncover it, so you'll need to be persistent and firm in your resolve.

Now, to determine the consequences of your assumptions (whether they are erroneous or realistic) you can continue the sequence with: ... and so ...?

For the son of the dentist who feels entitled to succeed by right of blood, the next irrational assumption might be: ...*And so I don't have to study and am free to party as much as I want.*

At this point, you'll be able to determine if you're viewing the future through a clear or a distorted lens, to anticipate the consequences of your thinking, and to make better longe-range decisions for yourself.

The more you practice this exercise the better your ability to uncover your hidden expectations. The answers to the questions will arise with greater ease and grow more detailed, like branches sprouting from the trunk of a tree. It may sound silly, but memorizing the thinking road map of If...then...because...and so can be very helpful when you are contemplating your choices in any problematic situation and reevaluating your goals.

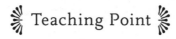

Teaching Point

THE JUDGING MIND

We all have one, and it has an opinion about pretty much everything. It is the voice of internal dialogue that lists all the rights and wrongs, good and bad, and tells us how things "should" be. Sometimes, it even judges its own tendency to judge. In the process of self-examination, the judging mind can be a great hindrance. The best means of defusing it is simply just to acknowledge it without being judgmental.

Recently a friend told me about how difficult it was for him to deal with people who talk on cell phones, particularly on buses. When he would overhear the conversation of passengers sitting near him, he would become angry and critical of their lack of consideration. He'd feel superior in his high regard for those much more polite and civilized individuals who did *not* chat on a cell phone in public.

My friend recognized that this attitude was, in fact, just his mind running off in its judging state, as it was prone to do. "So I watched it and didn't suppress it," he told me. "And when I saw how quick it was to insult others, the mind-set lost its pull."

There will be moments for all of us when we'll be free of the inner struggle with our judging voice and moments when we'll be caught in its grip. Sometimes the voice of the judging mind is loudest when it is directed at one's self, and these are the moments when it is essential to cultivate the powers of self-acceptance. To judge yourself negatively for being as you are is like judging the moon, the weather, and the sea for ebbing and surging tides. Being kind to yourself and aware of your nature opens you up to all the possible benefits of working through this book.

Using Stress for Personal Growth

The third step to inner peace is to acknowledge the reality of carrying burdens and pressures. Facing up to these challenges can be an opportunity to develop the courage and stamina needed to truly bring you your "heart's desire."

In today's world, nearly everyone complains about too much stress. We all rush to meet our obligations and the expectations we have of ourselves or that others may have of us. It can often feel as if there aren't enough hours in the day for all that we have to do. When we can't get everything done, when something blocks the way of our reaching our goals, frustration, anger, and anxiety arise. We get tense and bothered.

Every day, we interact with coworkers, classmates, and neighbors; fellow members of our church, synagogue, or mosque, of our club and gym; friends and family—and all of these associations can bring us support, companionship, love, and laughter. But they can also be fraught with non-acceptance, disrespect, and shame.

Life brings hardship, sickness, aging, and challenges beyond our ability to predict. Sometimes we are traumatized by losses, injuries, or catastrophes.

Yet, in the face of it all, it is still possible to maintain equanimity.

Stress is inevitable. Life is full of drama, trials, and tensions, which can often interfere with and even eclipse a sense of inner peace. The more dramatic—or traumatic—stress becomes, the more feelings of pessimism, hopelessness, and helplessness can arise.

Some stresses are within your control. Some are not. Some are paradoxical; they continue to arise, unbidden, in your thoughts as you try to push them away because of the unpleasant emotions they evoke. But you always have the choice of how to react to stress and how to think about it.

Every change, strain, or trauma, no matter how big or small, requires a shift in thinking, an assimilation of what has happened, and an adjustment. This skill to adapt can be learned and practiced by anyone with the openness for honest self-examination and a willingness to grow, learn, and change. The more self-aware you are, the more adept you can become at handling yourself, keeping your cool, weathering any storm, and becoming a stronger, wiser, better person.

Using your mind as a tool for exploring the most important past episodes and current circumstances of your life can lead to new revelations about yourself and how you relate to the world. It can help you attain new personal growth—a key factor for happiness. It can enhance your integration. It can change your character.

LET STRESS BE YOUR MOTIVATION

Page through any magazine or newspaper, and you're bound to come across an article on stress. And there's no shortage of books or TV talk shows to provide you with advice on how to manage and reduce it. This is all worthwhile information. Acute and chronic stress can be damaging to your physical and emotional health. Unrelenting, unrelieved stress needs to be taken seriously.

But not all stress is harmful. Imagine yourself skydiving, reaching the summit of a great mountain, standing at the altar to marry your beloved, becoming a first-time parent and bringing home your newborn infant, waiting behind the curtain as it's about to rise on opening night, negotiating a raise in salary, or chasing a breaking story that will make your career. These scenarios are all full of stress as well as chills, thrills, fun, and excitement. These are the types of experiences that keep us vital.

I define *stress* as any type of change that causes physical, emotional, or mental strain. Every new or unusual situation creates stress to some degree. Stress can stimulate us to think and act—to react quickly to situations. For prehistoric primates, the physical changes in response to stress were essential for meeting natural threats. In today's world, the stress response can raise performance levels in sports, business, or other circumstances of real danger or crisis. Stress can be useful: Transformed into productive and positive energy, it can take the boredom out of life. Even the stress and grief that follow separations and losses, while painful, can lead to growth in a sense of solid, capable identity and reduce preexisting views of self as a child rather than an adult.

On the other hand, a bad marriage, an extremely taxing, unrewarding job, or an isolated life of too much solitude—can result in the kind of stresses that seem never ending, inescapable, and sap the joy from living. Episodic stresses, such as an attack of road rage, a fight with your boss or a defiant child, an encounter with an extremely slow salesclerk or a rude stranger, or the loss of your expensive new eyeglasses, can also drain the serenity from the day in a nanosecond.

Some stressors are predictable and thus less inevitable. With a little forward thinking, you can prepare to avert or meet them. With maturity and a clear-lens view of yourself and your reality, you can avoid exaggerating or minimizing stressors because of some distorted assumption that you may be making.

In order to think clearly and truthfully about stressful topics, some degree of emotional distress is inevitable, but suffering in and of itself does not change anything. The gain is not in the pain but in learning that you have more tolerance for negative feelings than you previously thought and in what is derived from the discomfort: New insights and new approaches to living are reached. These gains are the silver lining of the dark, oppressive cloud.

THINKING IT THROUGH

Anyone who is trying to grow up and grow wiser must learn to tolerate negative feelings so he or she may tackle the lesson waiting to be learned. As you begin to examine your stress, you are likely to find yourself encountering obstacles to clarity. You can view these roadblocks as a source of great frustration or as your best chance to find your way to a breakthrough, by exploring them, learning to think through or around them, and coming to know their nature. It's all in how you see it.

Stressful events create an avalanche of thoughts.

For example, when twenty-five-year-old Harold, a software programmer, was fired from his job, he was stunned. He hadn't seen it coming and, caught off guard, he reeled from the news. As he left his office and headed home, his stomach churned, his jaw clenched, his skin flushed, and his thoughts raced. He was besieged by feelings of hurt, anger, embarrassment, resentment, and anxiety.

Why had he been fired? How had this happened? Who was to blame? Would his parents see this as another failure? How would his fiancée react? Where should he look for another job? How should he go about finding another position? How would he manage in the meantime?

These questions weren't easy to think about. And thinking about them all at once was overwhelming, sending Harold into a state of gut-wrenching confusion.

When hit with bad news, we all experience this rush

of highly emotional thinking. Our minds go over and over the event as we absorb the shock. This repetitive tendency is natural. With the cyclical thinking can come unbidden, uncomfortable images and sudden pangs of painful feelings. The inclination to inhibit, to stifle the emotion, can lead to numbness and denial. We all want to avoid negative emotions, so we tend to shift away from ideas, memories, and fantasies that generate them. We don't want to pour gasoline on the fire, so we may even introduce distortions into our thinking.

The mind can become a clutter of intrusive thoughts and avoidant efforts to "change the channel." Selecting one topic at a time for closer contemplation can counteract both extremes. Working on a stress episode means honestly examining and reconsidering your own traits.

As long as Harold's mind was spinning, he was caught in a rut with his pain. But when he focused his attention on why he was fired, he was able to arrive at a realistic reason. Then he could recall the moment he received the news of his dismissal without feeling the sharp and shocking sense of pain that he'd experienced the first time. He could ask and answer his many questions about being fired. He began to understand the episode and to make it an integrated part of his personal life story. After he had worked through all of his troubling thoughts, he found, like Belinda in the previous chapter, new freedom to choose how he would move forward.

THE DAILY GRIND

My field of expertise is in mastering all kinds of stressor events. Many of the men and women I see are under chronic stress, but not necessarily because of a catastrophic type of traumatic event or because they feel intense despair. Rather, they experience a passionless neutrality, or chronic boredom, or restlessness, or apathy. They seem to have the internal stress of unknown conflicts and too little satisfaction. They can't quite put a finger on why they aren't happy, and they find it equally hard to say what their goals are and how they realistically and patiently plan to achieve them.

This was the situation for Ronald, a successful self-made land developer, when he first consulted me about the possibility of entering therapy. At the time, he was forty-two, in a stable marriage, the father of two healthy, well-adjusted children, and the owner of a stately old house in a lovely neighborhood. Materially, financially, and in his personal life, he seemed to have reached the complete fulfillment of the American dream.

Yet Ronald wasn't happy. He rarely felt anxious or angry, he said. He was seldom troubled by confusion or depression. He was in great physical health. He just couldn't get enthusiastic about anything anymore, he explained to me, and he was running out of hope that he ever would. He'd come to see me to investigate if therapy might help him explain and address his arid emotional state.

I told him that I thought therapy could help him feel happier and decrease his boredom and restlessness. Our work together would be a journey of exploration, I explained. We'd identify his deepest values, beliefs, and priorities, and take a hard look at his goals and his actions to see if there were contradictions between them. We'd delve, too, into his vision of his future possibilities. I couldn't promise we'd achieve the desired result, but we could begin and see how it went.

Ronald asked intelligent questions. He also wanted to know how long this "fishing expedition" would go on and how much it would run him. I told him my fees. "I can't predict how long it will take or the total cost," I said, honestly, "but it's likely to take a while and to be expensive and your health insurance won't cover it."

Ronald quickly calculated that the tab would be in the thousands of dollars. "At these prices, I could be buying a yacht, paying it off month by month," he said, his face showing some animation for the first time since I'd met him.

"Perhaps you could buy a boat," I said, "but you've been telling me you have this steady sour feeling about your life, and here is the opportunity at hand for you to try to understand it and to get to know yourself better."

"No," Ronald replied, smiling broadly, looking genuinely jolly now, "a yacht is what I truly want. Thank you for showing me that I can afford it."

And that is where our consultation ended—until a year later, when Ronald called for an appointment.

"I really did enjoy the boat," he said, "but I'm willing to sell it now and pay for therapy. I'm still bored and restless a lot of the time. And some of the things you said about possible contradictions between my goals and my actions made sense to me. You also told me that if I tried I could become a 'man of substance'—something like that—and I keep thinking about that phrase. I'd like to try working with you to see if I can figure this out."

It took Ronald a year to come around to seeing the need to work on his integration, intimacy, and integrity issues, but he did get there, and it benefited him more in the long run than any other gift he could have given himself.

OVERCOMING SETBACKS

Sometimes, life can be terribly ugly. History has taught us that. And, sadly, many people learn the lesson first-hand, often in childhood. There is a spectrum in the life experience that runs from great evil to great love, from emotional chaos to calm serenity, and from agony to bliss. No one has the power to make his or her life *only* beautiful. We are all subject to the whims of fate. But through our choices as adults, we can pursue beauty and move away from agonies whenever possible.

There are some people who seem to have an innate capacity for optimism and resilience, while others despair easily if their lives are upset. Resilient individuals survive and even thrive in the face of a struggle. Fragile and fearful folks crumble. Most of us fall somewhere in between, but with work and greater self-knowledge, we can all become more adept at bouncing back and riding more smoothly through the challenges that life sends our way.

I'm sure there will be readers who may argue that their pursuit of happiness is enormously influenced by the circumstances of childhood, family, culture, economic status, good or bad luck, disease, disability, age, chemical imbalances, or genes. I agree that there are circumstances and physical and emotional wounds that alter lives forever. Natural disasters, such as hurricanes, tornados, mudslides, and fires, and personal disasters, such as illness and the death of a spouse or a child, forever rearrange the world for those who survive. These are soul-wounding events. But I have seen how people can attain or maintain happiness in spite of these influences.

Resilience and inner peace and harmony are not only about overcoming hardships and tragedies. They are not only about what to do when the house collapses. They are about how you build the foundation of your mature self in the first place. I have seen men and women become "people of substance," able to weather the storms of their lives because they have worked to build strength of character, integrity, maturity, and wisdom within themselves.

My patient Alice falls into this category.

ALICE: THE ART OF OVERCOMING SETBACKS

Alice's troubles began while she was still in high school. At eighteen, she had an unwanted pregnancy. Terminating the pregnancy simply wasn't an option for her and her boyfriend, Todd. Instead, they decided to marry, and a few months after their graduation, little Annie was born. Following the wedding, Todd began working as a freelance carpenter, while Alice stayed home to care for the baby. Their earnings were meager, which, of course, contributed to Alice's sense of being heavily burdened by responsibilities. But she adored her baby, and she loved Todd.

Alice couldn't swing the time or expense of college, but she was able to work with a family member to develop some basic business skills. When Todd got a contractor's license, Alice handled advertising for him and hired helpers. Together, they began building a small business; and their income improved.

Five years later, however, Todd ran away with another woman, leaving a note that told Alice she could have the business and all of their belongings. Alice wasn't all that sorry. Todd had been drinking heavily, and she'd been contemplating a separation anyway. But things went from bad to worse very quickly for her. The business dissolved almost immediately and couldn't be sold. While the divorce she'd initiated was in process, there was no income, and Todd couldn't be located for child support. Alice and her daughter moved in with Alice's uncle.

"It was the lowest point in my life," Alice recalled later. "Some days, I just wanted to go to sleep and not wake up. I felt totally hopeless."

With all that Alice was going through, it's easy to understand why she might have lost hope. Still, she had no way of knowing what her future held. Imagine Tom

Hanks, stranded on an island in the middle of a vast ocean, or Sigourney Weaver, the sole survivor on a spaceship overrun by aliens, repeatedly saying to themselves "It's totally hopeless. I want to just go to sleep and not wake up."

In movies, the audience easily accepts that the greater the crisis, the more dire the circumstances, the more opportunity there is for a hero or heroine to triumph. In real life, however, it's another story. When you suffer a defeat or a setback, it's easy to fall into despair, to believe you are lost, not just for the moment but forever. Like Alice, you may forget that the story of your life is ongoing, continuing to unfold, and still full of infinite opportunities. Anything is possible.

It's also especially hard to persevere and keep hope alive if you grew up in a broken home, with a mother who was emotionally volatile and unable to keep a job, and you had no expectation that the situation would improve; which was the case for Alice, who had never been able to count on her father, either. He'd had a gambling addiction and appeared in her life only occasionally, when he was on a winning streak and could slip her a few dollars before disappearing again, sometimes for months at a time. Alice had good reason to be pessimistic as a child.

Now, however, at twenty-three, she needed to stop viewing the world from the perspective of a dependent little girl. She had a lot of life to be lived, and the quality of her future depended on her seeing her situation through a clearer lens.

Desperate times can bring out the best in people and

overcoming hardship requires strong character to reach within to find the way out. In her darkest hour, Alice had the emotional courage to look beyond her hopelessness. She didn't sidestep the many difficult questions that churned in her mind but began to sift through them one by one.

How could she handle her anger? How could she let go of her desire to get even with her deserting husband? How much of the failure of her marriage had been her fault? How much might her behavior have provoked the separation? Was she still a desirable woman? Would there ever be another man in her life? Did she even want that? Was she capable of raising a child alone? Was she providing enough good mothering to her daughter? Was it wrong to feel angry and frustrated at Annie sometimes for being a burden? Was she placing an unfair burden on her uncle? Was she grateful enough to him? Was it right to borrow money from him to go to school? How much would that increase her sense of obligation and dependency? Could she ever earn a good income? What kind of career should she seek? How skillful could she become? Would she be able to stick with it?

These were important questions for Alice. Finding clarity about all these issues was her path to regaining her equilibrium and achieving personal growth, but the first step was asking the questions and knowing that there was no way the answers were going to come to her quickly or easily. She viewed them as a big loaf of bread: taking one slice at a time and letting the other slices wait for later.

For everyone facing a sudden crisis or dealing with an ongoing dilemma, thinking about stressful questions will go on and on, either in murky or clear ways, and it is very tempting to ignore the nagging queries when answers don't come easily, solutions are elusive, and uncomfortable emotions arise. Of course, it's easier to put them out of mind and find a more pleasant diversion, but they'll come back again and again until there is some kind of resolution.

Alice reaped the rewards of her hard work. After much contemplation, she decided she could borrow money from her uncle for her education. Over the next two years, she went to a community college, studied computer technology, showed a talent for programming, and eventually landed a job at a computer company. Soon, she was able to begin paying back her uncle and providing more easily for herself and Annie. Quite quickly, she rose to a mid-level position as a software developer. One night, while attending an activity at Annie's school, she met Katherine, another divorced mom who was raising a child alone. The two women became good friends and in time decided to rent an apartment together and share the costs and responsibilities of child care.

"We're a can-do survival team, a dynamic duo of moms," Alice now likes to say.

Alice had clearly found her way to a new, better chapter of her life with a greater and more solid sense of happiness than she'd ever known before.

REALISTIC THINKING AND AUTHENTIC HOPE

Alice's realistic choices and her faith in the future were keys to her success in increasing her self-organization (integration) by deciding on her personally selected priorities; her new friendships confirmed in her a readiness for intimacy; and her disciplined sequence of actions assured her that she was acting with integrity. But she didn't get there easily. It took hard work, courage, an openness to ask and answer difficult questions, the patience to wait for answers, and a belief that time would bring new solutions and opportunities. Curbing impatience, knowing that states of mind fluctuate, and trusting in time and repetitive effort are the three biggest lessons in Alice's journey.

Once upon a time, Alice had wanted to be a singer, but she recognized that to follow that teenage dream would have been a poor choice. She realized that it wouldn't have been wise, either, for her to devote a lot of effort in search of a new romance, although she wanted to find love again someday. And she was also savvy enough to know that pursuing all of her objectives simultaneously would have been too great a drain on her time and energy. By prioritizing her goals and tackling them step by step, Alice empowered herself and found her way to happiness.

When Todd left her, Alice experienced a very grim state of mind: She was depressed, feeling worthless and incompetent, and was unable to sustain her trains of thought. Her future seemed hopeless. Every tiny dream in her heart seemed doomed to failure even before she began. What was the point? In her depressed state she was telling herself: *I will always be in this state.* But this thinking isn't realistic; no state of mind lasts forever.

When Alice acknowledged her depression, she made a small yet very important shift. By simply naming her mood and acknowledging that she wasn't likely to always feel this way, she lifted her morale. Her changed theory, which she did not quite believe at first, made all the difference.

This can work for everyone. It's a lesson that many fairy tales teach. We've all heard it: Keep your chin up, be patient, endure, wait, roll up your sleeves, get to work, and realistically good things can happen, if not now, then later. Simply by naming a mood, you gain a little bit of control over it. I call this technique "controlling your states of mind." Once you identify a state of mind, you can acknowledge its transience and thereby gain a little bit of hope.

For Alice it was the turning point, the beginning of her struggle to living more happily. This spark of hope allowed her to address the difficult issues that arose in her mind, one by one, dose by dose, piece by piece, one step forward, half a step back and then forward again. If Alice had demanded an answer to every question in one sitting, she would have become frustrated and set in the negative attitudes of her depression. But she was able to curb her impatience and put a little trust in time and repetitive effort. She focused on the near future with as hopeful an attitude as she could muster. She considered short- and long-term goals. She sorted out her values and determined her immediate priorities.

Although she was married and a mother, Alice was young and inexperienced, and beneath her depression she had a lot of potential energy. She grew from adolescent to adult attitudes—a passage everyone needs to make to find true happiness. Her story is one example of how exploring the deeper layers of the self leads to a lasting equanimity.

CENTERING, DECENTERING, AND RECENTERING

I have heard a piece of useful advice repeated frequently: Be your own best friend. That phrase condenses a lot:

- Give yourself a sympathetic rather than critical ear even when you are hearing a lot of complaints.
- Give yourself useful advice that comes from knowing both your strengths and your weaknesses.
- Care about how your future might unfurl.
- And more.

To be your own confidant means decentering from yourself as the person thinking your thoughts and feeling your feelings. You move to an alternate point of view on those complex and sometimes knotted networks of ideas and emotions. Even on a seemingly single topic, like what to do on a free, unplanned day, from the other, decentered-on-me point of view, you may sort out the mix somewhat differently. Decentering can help you attain clarity on possible decisions.

Some temporary mental tricks can help the decentering, and the tricks are dropped when you recenter on yourself as the real agent of your actions. Here is a list:

- Imagine you are a wise, experienced, and admired character, even one from fiction. Imagine that character listening and commenting on you, or write a letter "from" them to you. "Dear John, you are still smarting from that insult when Joe said that he was surprised a spacey guy like you would get the promotion. How long are you going to replay that tape? Why not just walk ahead and leave that well behind you?"
- Put an empty chair a few feet away, facing you. Chairs are pretty good at symbolizing people. You can talk to the chair, and then go sit on that chair and talk back to your chair.
- Imagine you are your future self and write a commentary about how you are "now." Ten years later you can reflect more clearly on your current conundrum.
- Imagine you are a good parent advising a younger person having the current dilemma. Imagine the inner thought process of that parent who wants the very best for you. How does that good parent sift though your various possibilities and probabilities? "I think he may be obsessed with fame and glory. I hope he doesn't decide to put all his time and energy into being a virtuoso drummer but that

he balances that interest with other activities, like finding a steady day job and a girlfriend."

THE CASE OF MARY

A middle-aged individual facing a life crisis is likely to confront a more complex set of issues.

When Mary was widowed—her husband, Henry, died from leukemia after three years of a difficult fight—she had two children to raise alone: a boy, seven, and a girl, nine. As a young, single woman, Mary had wanted to teach physical education in high school or college, and she had earned a master's degree. But after she'd fallen in love with Henry and they married, she'd devoted herself to their home and children. Henry was a lawyer who'd made a good living, and Mary hadn't needed to work. After Henry's death, Mary's financial picture changed, but she had enough money from insurance and investments to support her children and herself, if she was frugal.

Mary's mother wanted Mary and the children to move across the country and live in her home. Mary didn't want to do that. She suggested that her mother come to live with them. Mary's mother refused. They argued and the fight escalated, leaving bitter feelings on both sides. Mary had no other close family. Her father, who had divorced her mother many years earlier, was no longer alive. Except for a few close women friends, Mary was alone.

Mary's marriage had been loving and happy. She could envision finding intimacy with another man again, sometime. But with two young children, in the midst of intense grief, facing the challenge of reconstructing her life, it wasn't likely that there would be any chance of romance for her in the near future.

Like Alice, Mary had many questions to confront. But unlike Alice, Mary had the maturity to sort out her options and choose her goals with greater self-awareness and confidence. She decided that her children were her top priority. Caring for them was more important than any of her personal or professional aspirations.

Mary did, however, decide that there was room in her life for her to continue her creative pursuits. For several years, she'd been part of a semiprofessional dance company. She made no money from the performances, but now she looked at her involvement with the company as an opportunity to hone her skills in choreography and develop experience as a dance teacher, which might, in time, lead to a new career.

A few months later, Mary went to a nearby community college and proposed to the administration that she teach a single dance class. She was paid a very tiny stipend. But by maintaining focus on her goal, she put in place a step-by-step plan. Over the next few years, she made connections at the college, increased the number of classes she taught, and eventually persuaded the school authorities to establish within the physical education program a dance department, which she directed.

Within five years, Mary was staging performances in

the college's auditorium, and the dance department grew to have three faculty members. She also gained local acclaim as a choreographer.

Ten years after Henry's death, with her career on track and her children in their teens, Mary was finally ready to begin dating again. She soon met a man who seemed to offer her everything she was looking for in a partner. She took her courtship with him very slowly, insisted on a long engagement, and then enjoyed planning a big, beautiful wedding that was very different from the small private ceremony in which she and Henry had been married. Mary's second time around at love turned out to be as happy and rewarding as her first.

When tragedy struck Mary's life, she had been left in drastically changed circumstances, on her own, solely responsible for two young children, with no guarantees or certainty about her future. But she knew her priorities. Her children came first. Second came developing a source of income by doing relatively well at something she liked. Third, although it took a decade, was pursuing opportunities for another intimate relationship. As a new widow, Mary had been deeply wounded and frightened, but she was still secure enough in her own judgment to know she did not want to uproot her children from their familiar neighborhood and move thousands of miles away to live in a seemingly safer situation with her mother. She stood by her decision, even when it meant fighting with her mother.

Putting the pieces of her life in this firm order of importance and forging ahead alone had its consequences.

Mary had to work hard and make many sacrifices to live on a strict budget. She needed great patience and focus to establish a place for herself as a professional. She was somewhat lonely. But her life was filled with activities. Her children were secure, well cared for, and well adjusted. And ultimately, she found great happiness and success after a long journey through grief.

Thanks to her self-awareness, values, integrity, and emotional maturity, Mary was able to master and triumph over her stressful circumstances. Hers are the qualities and coping skills that everyone needs to chart a course through the upsets of daily living, past the difficult dilemmas, beyond even the most grievous injuries of the past. These are the cornerstones of character—and the good news is they can be developed by anyone who is willing to adopt new attitudes and new actions.

THE EYE OF THE BEHOLDER

Individuals experience stress differently—one person's source of pressure, strain, and discomfort can be another's great pleasure and stimulation, and vice versa. It might seem that the stress of failure would be universal. But in some circumstances, failure is a relief. For example, a young student who entered dental school only to please his parents may be quite glad to flunk out. *Now I can do what I want next,* he might think, in spite of facing anxiety from disappointing his parents and from having no plans in place for his future.

Success can cut both ways, too. Aside from the increased responsibilities and time pressures that success may bring, stress can occur because the reality of success fails to meet expectations. A newly appointed manager of a corporation, for instance, might have unrealistically expected that all the people he supervised would love, admire, and respect him, be pleased to accept his authority, and grateful to absorb his plans and direction. The actual and much more likely outcome might be that he'd gain some respect, power, and control, but it would also cost him companionship, because he was no longer an equal among his peers. And it might bring him some anger and resentment from his colleagues, who could have mixed feelings about his promotion, perhaps because they wanted the position themselves, or because they were afraid he had power over them. So instead of the glory that the new manager expected to bask in, he would be steeped in a bitter brew of seeming admiration that really masked ambivalence—a long way from what he thought would be his dream come true.

In both cases, there's something to be learned. If the new manager and the failed student were to examine the thoughts and feelings behind their circumstances, they each might find their way to viewing their own hopes and fears, their own skills and shortcomings, their own values with a clearer lens. Their stress could be their greatest teacher, pointing them to the pursuit of true and lasting happiness, not being sidetracked by compromised or unrealistic goals and expectations.

A Supplementary Lesson:
Be Careful What You Wish For

History and literature are filled with examples of men, women, heroes, heroines, and villains who have lost much more than they gained while seeking to achieve their greatest desire. One of the best-known fictional characters to seek his happiness by having his greatest wish fulfilled is Faust, who first appeared in the seventeenth century in a play by Christopher Marlowe and in two books by German author Johann Wolfgang von Goethe. In these works, Dr. Faust is a university professor, one of the most learned men of his time, but in spite of his great knowledge, he's bored and restless. His life of learning seems without meaning. So he uses his skill to call up Satan, who offers him a deal: The professor will live until he experiences the ultimate pinnacle of satisfaction, and then Satan will claim his soul. Faust agrees to the bargain.

Faust's first desire is to have sex with a beautiful virgin. So the devil makes a magnificent young woman fall in love with old Faust. But that love leads to pregnancy and scandal, and Faust, who's grown to love the young woman, experiences terrible anguish. In Goethe's second book, Faust, having learned that neither his scholarly achievements nor his carnal satisfactions have brought him fulfillment, seeks happiness by serving others. He uses his knowledge to direct the building of levees, to protect low-lying fields from flooding, thereby improving crops and feeding a famished population. Standing on a hill, overlooking all that he has accomplished, Faust has his experience of bliss: "May this moment endure, for it is so beautiful," he proclaims.

But since the deal is now consummated, Satan takes Faust's soul, and he is in anguish once again. In later Hollywood versions, a happy ending is inserted. Heaven intervenes to reward Faust's goodness. As we note, the moral is not "Don't make deals with the devil," but pay attention to your own service to others.

Also, what you imagine your desire will bring may not be what you get.

In modern times and in the real world, the experience of former president Richard Nixon is another cautionary tale of the gap between the fantasy of desire and the reality of wishes fulfilled. Nixon was a clever, determined, and persistent politician. He ultimately became one of the most powerful men in the world. But, according to biographers, living in the White House wasn't at all what he'd imagined. He'd thought guards dressed in livery would surround him. He'd envisioned soldiers in uniforms like those of the Swiss guards who protected the pope in Rome. He questioned if he was being denied these symbols of awe and respect because he was a Republican. Would a Democratic president be treated differently, he wondered? He was assured this was not the case.

Nixon grew increasing distrustful of people around

him. He believed there were conspiracies at work, determined to undermine him. He had only a close team of a very few allies. Together, they spied on anyone of whom the president was suspicious. Also, according to reports, Nixon lit fires in the Oval Office even in hot weather, in order to cheer himself up. Nixon had achieved his greatest ambition—to be president—but he clearly was not a happy man.

Teaching Points

- One way to happiness lies in mastery of stressors. It's not what you suffer, but how you deal with suffering.
- Work to develop skills of mind so as to see reality clearly, without distortions, so the assumptions you make, conclusions you draw, and decisions you reach are sound.
- The integration of all your self-concepts provides a sturdy base for developing a calm, centered maturity. By developing harmony within yourself, you will grow up, grow wise, and find a constant and grounded center from which to cope with new circumstances.
- Simply by naming a mood, control is gained over it. Once a state of mind is identified, it can be acknowledged that it is not always going to be present— and a little bit of hope can be born.

PART TWO

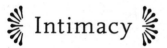 Intimacy

Connecting to the World

Maintaining closeness and harmony in romantic relationships, families, and friendships requires emotional maturity and navigational skills to steer through the inevitable tensions and strains that arise in even the happiest affiliations

The quality of our lives is greatly influenced by the quality of our relationships. When relationships work, life can be joyful; when relationships *don't* work, life can feel like a grind. Frustration and resentment can lead to pointless arguments with romantic partners, colleagues, friends, and family members. We might feel trapped, bitter, caught in repeating patterns of behavior, and at a loss for what to do. Or we might be so distant that we feel lonely and isolated.

We all need to be connected to the world. The more we are part of a community in which we feel understood, valued, and accepted, the greater our chances for contentment. Maintaining long-term, close associations increases our happiness in life. And, of course, almost all of us dream of falling in love and remaining united with a life partner on a mutually shared, cherished, and harmonious path through the years, to be separated only by death. Alas, few of us attain such high and enduring levels of peaceful intimacy.

We all have varying degrees of tolerance for solitude. Some individuals can be quite content to work under isolated conditions. However, I don't fall into this category, as I discovered the summer I worked for the U.S. Fish and Wildlife Service in Alaska, guarding salmon streams from poachers.

That summer, apart from a service seaplane that visited me once a week with provisions and mail, I was alone as I had never been alone before. I had no radio and few books, or other diversions. My loneliness was acute and painful, but it served as a powerful catalyst to start me thinking about my life.

One afternoon, several weeks after I'd arrived in Alaska, I had an experience that led to a profoundly significant insight for me. I'd moored my boat on a low tide and walked out across the exposed bottom of the bay to examine the interesting terrain, stretching for miles. Then, when the tide began to flood back in, I turned to return to my boat. I'd been careful not to walk too far away from it. I'd considered the safety factor. But I'd miscalculated.

The tide came in much more quickly than I'd expected. It inched up my thigh-high rubber boots— fast. I kept slogging back toward my boat, but the going was slow and difficult. Then it got worse. A wave washed over the top of my boots, filling them with painfully cold water. The walking was far too slow. The thought occurred to me that this was a truly dangerous situation. I could drown. I could disappear to be crab food. Heart pounding, I pulled off my boots and parka and started swimming to my boat.

Thoroughly scared and filled with self-criticism—how could I have been so foolish?—I made it to the boat a few minutes later. Climbing aboard, I retrieved my floating clothes and, motoring back to shore, I thought about the letters I'd received the previous day from three good friends and how much I just wanted to reread the letters and write back. Later, sitting by my fire, I considered what had happened to me a "near-death experience." I was even more frightened afterward than I had been during the ordeal, although I was uninjured, except for my pride.

I missed people *desperately*, and the admission of this fact filled my consciousness. I realized, deep inside, in a way in which I'd never experienced the knowledge before, that relationships were one of my most important priorities. My happiness depended on being connected to others. It was a simple truth to discover, but a vital realization for me. In the years to come, this self-knowledge would be a crucial factor in many of my decisions. The image of lapping water, being terrified, and swimming through the rising tide to reach safety has remained etched in my mind. It is a symbol of one of my most important truths: Relationships are vital to me.

We all have a history that includes relationships with others. As babies, our first, most important caregivers provide a blueprint for our intimate relationships. Other role models supply more templates as we grow, but the early formative patterns of social behavior that we develop live on, becoming part of our mature, complex sense of identity. Our earliest schemas might be reworked many times to form later patterns, but nothing is erased; the old, outmoded models remain dormant, subordinated into inactivity. No two brains are exactly alike, even in identical twins, and every individual finds unique configurations of relationship models. In other words, we all have different, many-layered, mental maps for interacting with others.

Many of us also have fears of intimacy that may be conscious or unconscious and that may prevent us from truly experiencing the interconnections we crave. The most common fears are:

1. Being trapped in a "wrong choice" relationship that will prevent you from living the life you truly desire.
2. Being overpowered, controlled, or dominated by another.
3. Being merged into a union that will eclipse your identity.
4. Worry that your significant other will change into a nag, burden, drain, or albatross.
5. Worry that you will "smother" or be smothered by a significant other.
6. Worry that you will become overly dependent, needing the other person so much that you cannot stand the possibility of losing him or her.

7. Worry that once you are attached, your needs and wishes will not be met, and you will become hopelessly enraged and/or abandoned.
8. All of the above.

If you recognize that you harbor one or more of these fears, chances are you can find a reason for it. For many of us, intimacy can seem just too risky because experience has shown us that it isn't safe to be become deeply attached to another. Perhaps your parents' marriage was fraught with tension. Perhaps your father hit your mother or browbeat her into submission, and you identified with your mother's vulnerability. All your life, you've feared that you could be victimized in the same way if you gave your heart to another. Or maybe you identified with your dad's strength, and you've worried that someday you might be violent and aggressive with someone who is weaker. Later, if your father brought gifts and begged forgiveness, you might have seen your mom as strong and your dad as weak. Whatever the case, this sequence is very likely to have left you confused about what to expect from intimacy.

Even if your experience has been much less dramatic, you still grew up with expectations about intimacy, and our expectations are most often where our troubles begin. For instance, we might subscribe to a "storybook ideal": We imagine a perfect romance to be the fulfillment of all our dreams. At the other extreme, we might anticipate a worst-case scenario. We also might secretly believe that we are not worthy of love or fear that we'll be abandoned or disappear into an unfulfilling role. Relationships are too hard, we may think. "Together forever" is an impossible dream.

Yet many couples achieve it. Many men and women find the middle ground of the more realistic interpretation. They identify the extremes in their thinking, admit the irrationality of fantasy, the unlikelihood of certain disaster, and clarify a temperate, real-life view that falls somewhere in between.

PHIL: THE CYCLE OF BROKEN RELATIONSHIPS

Phil was twenty-three when he met Angela at his first job out of college. He was a computer programmer. She was a sales consultant. They married after a short, joyful courtship and settled into happy domesticity. A few months after the wedding, however, Phil became mildly depressed and anxious, states of mind that he'd experienced before. This time, he decided to explore his troubled emotions in therapy and came to see me.

Naturally, we examined his circumstances, history, self-concepts, and perspectives on life and the world. In one early session, he told me about a disturbing evening that he'd had at home alone. Angela had gone to a party with her fellow sales consultants and some prospective buyers. Phil had remained home to watch a baseball game. While sitting in front of his television, he'd become more and more agitated, experiencing what therapists call an "episode of internal stress." He was looking at the sports channel, but his mind was churning. He was picturing Angela at her party, flirting with another man. A jealous anger rose in Phil. His thoughts rushed on. He visualized confronting her when she came home, writing the script in his head for an ugly scene that unleashed his fury at her and ended with him leaving her because of her infidelity.

Phil was an intelligent man. He knew he was conjuring a fantasy, not a real betrayal. He knew that it was inappropriate to want Angela to involve him in one hundred percent of her life interests. She had every right to go to a party alone. He shouldn't have a problem with staying home to watch a sporting event that she found boring. Yet he was clearly upset by her going out socially on her own.

When Angela returned, he restrained himself from saying anything about what had been on his mind. She was glad to see him. She reported on the party and spoke quite proudly about a compliment she'd received from a colleague. She wanted to share her experience with him, relive the pleasure. It was clear to Phil that Angela was perfectly okay with socializing without him. She felt no remorse at having left him alone. She certainly didn't see them as companions who were fused together in everything.

Yet Phil couldn't shake the sullen mood that had overcome him. He couldn't quite rouse himself to respond to Angela with genuine warmth. He realized he'd wanted her to show at least some regret for having left him alone all evening. They went to bed that night without much more conversation.

This experience was an opportunity for Phil to investigate his expectations about marriage. When he dug deep, he came to realize as he hadn't before that he believed falling in love and marrying would entitle him to live "happily ever after." As a husband, he would always be blissful and calm. It was an unconscious, idealized fantasy and an unrealistic extreme. In his mind, he and Angela were lovebirds, perched side by side, living only for each other, oblivious to all others.

When Angela flew from this cage, her departure activated in Phil the other extremity of his beliefs, also unconscious, of the dreaded sad ending. From this mindset, Phil saw himself abandoned and lonely, and therefore rightfully furious, sullen, and resentful. This led to anger, fantasies of retaliation and revenge against Angela, and then, ultimately, to losing her.

Between his idealized and dreaded sets of expectations, Phil had a more realistic attitude. In this rational view, separations from his wife were transitory, acceptable, and unthreatening. When he and Angela were apart, there was no reason to be angry.

Phil's unconscious expectations were there to snare him, making him vulnerable to repeating a pattern of broken relationships. Like a play in three acts, his mindsets were linked and flowed into one another.

ACT ONE: Lonely boy meets lovely girl and falls in love. The lovebird ideal is activated.

ACT TWO: Boy fears losing girl. An event occurs that feels like abandonment, and fear escalates. The boy gets upset when left alone, sees this as a betrayal, and becomes angry.

ACT THREE: The fight scene. Boy speaks harshly, abusively to girl. Girl, hurt and confused, rejects boy for real. Relationship over. Now the lonely boy is poised to meet another lovely girl...and the cycle repeats until the boy becomes a woman-hating man.

This is a life plan that is in need of change when you see it through a clear lens!

Phil was caught in this sequence. He now could see that he had been through it before with previous girlfriends. In this first enactment of it with Angela, Act Three entailed merely going to bed in sullen silence. But if his negative fantasies continued, never understood, if in the future more events of this type triggered him to act out of his roiling emotion, and if he became nasty enough toward her, his anger could have precipitated a real disruption in their relationship, eventually perhaps destroying their marriage.

This pattern is not uncommon. We're all susceptible to it. The bad cycle has to be uncovered to avoid the unhappy outcome. Professional counselors call this process of thinking about things reflectively a "differentiation" of past fantasies and current realities. When you undertake this work independently, you need to carefully consider the patterns of interaction that you have engaged in, in the past. Ask yourself: What thoughts and fantasies have directed your view of relationships? How might you redraw your conceptual map to better resemble the reality of the world you live in today or could create in the future?

I want to emphasize again the importance of taking time to do this well. Appraisal and reappraisal is a repetitive process. It starts slow, but the blessing is that it goes increasingly faster as you learn how to learn about yourself. Your best problem-solving tool is consciousness: being aware of your own patterns of thinking and their consequences in the moment, acknowledging your feelings but also keeping your emotions in check so that you may engage in reasoned contemplation.

Exercise: Clarifying Expectations About Intimacy

STEP 1: Identify any idealized, unrealistic, or extreme views you may hold.

Write them down. It is significantly helpful to see them on paper.

If you believe that you will live happily ever after when you meet the one person who is meant just for you, that you will be lifted up and carried away on a magic carpet, it will hurt like crazy when you are dropped back to earth. The only way to avoid the pain and lingering ache is to give up the romantic fantasy and find your happiness in reality. There is nothing wrong with a romantic high—the exhilaration of falling in love is wonderful— but you have to know it can't last. A long future of joy must be built on a much more solid foundation.

STEP 2: Identify any dreaded, unrealistic, or extreme views of a catastrophic outcome.

Do you believe, as one woman I know does, that marrying a man ultimately turns the wife into a drained caregiver? Do you agree with Henry Higgins that to let a woman in your life is to be constantly criticized and told what to do? Do you worry that you will be smothered in a relationship or not have enough control? Again, it's important to clarify these expectations in writing. Your list will be private, for your eyes only. You can throw it away at any time, but by seeing a hard-copy record of your irrational views, you increase your awareness of the danger of these worries provoking unwanted moods and unwanted behaviors, and, in turn, even provoking your significant other.

STEP 3: Clarify a temperate, realistic, nonextreme view.

The most important prerequisite for intimacy in all relationships—including casual acquaintances, close friendships, and family connections—is a sense of mutuality, a primal awareness of understanding and being understood. The closer you come to achieving a relationship based on realistic expatiations, the more mutually satisfying and fulfilling your relationship will be. The more you understand what underlies your communication—what motivates you to speak and act and what might be withheld—the more you will be able to see the world clearly and make better choices.

DEVELOPING A CAPACITY FOR INTIMACY

We don't all arrive at adulthood with the same capacity for intimacy. From infancy onward there are differences in how we each relate to others. When we look back into the past, we can learn lessons that can help guide our choices in the future. A general understanding of how intimacy develops may help clarify how your prior experiences shaped your interpretations and attitudes toward close associations and aid you in revising your patterns for interacting.

Infancy: We are all born with innate differences in personality and temperament, but we are also influenced from our first moments of life by experience. If a baby's needs are met, the lesson learned is that others can be trusted. In contrast, a baby who is poorly cared for may become anxious and fearful, feel abandoned, and so perhaps go through phases of anger, desperation, and/or apathy. This baby is very likely to become a child who is easily frightened and timid of strange situations. Fragility of trust may lead to adult problems with self-esteem.

But remember this: The developing mind is not a bag of concrete. It doesn't solidify and set forever. Later experiences and relationships can modify initially developed attitudes about the self and others and can compensate for and correct expectations that were formed by early traumas.

Childhood: As the emerging self develops, a child experiments with relationships through trial and error. In an optimal situation, when there is a close bond with a caring, loving parental figure, both negative and positive experiences provide lessons. A little boy or girl observes how others interact and tries copying behaviors to see what happens: He or she learns to give and mimic affection, to cheat or to tell the truth, to share, compete, or cooperate. Some children learn steadfastness and loyalty; others develop a tendency to sever a connection with another when a relationship hits a snag. Children follow rules, break them, and test the limits. The resulting responses and consequences provide the first road signs on the developing mental maps for intimacy.

Parents shape behavior with rewards and punishments. They encourage the best development when they criticize an unwanted behavior without implying that their child is a bad person, recognizing that an act of naughtiness may have bad consequences, without attacking, belittling, or calling their son or daughter derogatory names because of it. When parents are careful to make this distinction, kids learn early that good people sometimes behave badly, but there are remedies to compensate for transgressions. Some children, however, encounter harsh treatment when they misbehave. They are told that they are stupid, evil, unworthy, or degraded and made to feel responsible for hurting others.

Children who are emotionally, physically, and/or sexually abused often believe (because they've been taught or they assume) that their innate "badness" has caused their terrible circumstances. A child also might sometimes be faulted simply for asking to have his or her

needs met and from then onward have difficulty expressing wishes. He or she may even feel unentitled to live out
a heartfelt dream.

It is the nature of children to break rules and test the
waters for the effects of lying and deceit. Children are
also self-centered. Early on, we all need to learn about
causes and consequences of conflicts with our parents and
in the broader social context. Intimacy requires an understanding of clear boundaries and the skills of explanation, negotiation, and empathy for others. At one point or
another almost all children may hit a parent, pinch, or say
"I hate you!" Ideally, a parent will calmly explain why
this behavior is unacceptable and discuss other ways to
find solutions to problems and cope with frustrations. In
this way, a child learns the value of consideration and the
necessity of compromise between personal wants and the
needs of others, encouraging self-expression in a manner
that does not disrupt intimacy. Not all children get treated
so wisely, however. Some get blamed in ways that might
generate more hostility and create buried rage.

Children who are overloaded with blame handle their
stress by learning to extrude blame and hate on the world.
Deep down, maybe in an unconscious layer, they still
feel themselves to be "bad" and compensate by finding
others to blame. They may engage in strong vindictive
and impulsive acts, commit hate crimes, justifying and
rationalizing their position because they were deprived,
traumatized, or treated unjustly. Or they may respond
instead by withdrawing, becoming remote, and feeling
depressed. The self-talk that runs through their minds

may include persistent irrational attitudes toward and concepts of themselves and others. Should they project these onto their relationships, they can become self-fulfilling prophecies of bad outcomes.

Children are like scientists, developing theories about the consequences of their actions and how these actions affect intimacy. However, unlike scientists, they are not striving for objectivity and proof; thus their theories can be fantasies as well as realities. Whether stemming from a healthy perception or one based on hurt or other distortions, these theories can cast long shadows into the future.

Adolescence: With explosive shifts in their states of mind, teenagers are often likely to be ruled by impulses, but they are mature enough to begin to state their beliefs, to debate, philosophize, think, and talk more about human interactions and relationships. Close alliances with peers are significant to self-esteem at this age. Teens form cliques in which issues of acceptance and rejection become very important. A young person who doesn't achieve popularity with the so-called "in crowd" can engage in self-blame and self-loathing, or he or she can learn to successfully deal with rejection. A teen who appreciates the value of friendship can make the intellectual and moral choice to stick with a buddy who is ostracized. Being able to tolerate the stress and hurt of rejection, to stand up and do the right thing if a situation calls for it indicates a healthy developing capacity for intimacy.

Role models are very important to adolescents. Parents, grandparents, teachers, siblings, peers, as well as fictional characters all play a significant role in helping the developing young person learn to cope with the stresses of life, such as being rejected or feeling the pressure of expectations, and understanding how to face and deal with moral dilemmas. A teen needs to learn good values, to acquire confidence while interacting with others, and to develop skills for handling conflict within a cooperative and/or competitive sphere. An adolescent who hasn't learned to harmonize self-serving aims (such as being the best or winning admiration) and we-serving aims (sharing activities and glories and defeats) will find it hard to stay for long in an intimate friendship or love affair.

Adolescents also often experiment with sexuality, discovering the differences between lust and love. Young people date, break up, move on, and learn to engage in supportive relationships. The patterns or interactions that are established in these years will influence the future, either enhancing or impeding an individual's willingness to risk adult intimacy later.

JEFF: OVERCOMING ADOLESCENT TRAUMA

At fourteen, Jeff was on a thrilling ride. He and his girlfriend, Molly, went from playing doctor to engaging in sexual intercourse. Each encounter was exhilarating and enthralling, but after several weeks, Jeff's enthusiasm began to wane. Molly had come to need all of his attention, resenting the time he spent with his buddies, berating him if he took a few hours to play sports. When she began to call in the middle of the night, telling him to come to her at once "or else," Jeff felt overwhelmed. When he tried pulling back from her, Molly threatened suicide. One night, she sounded so desperate that Jeff felt compelled to run to her house. He climbed into her bedroom through a window and found her with blood flowing down her arm.

She had cut her skin with a razor blade. The wound was superficial. Jeff knew she wasn't in danger of bleeding to death, yet he was terrified. While Molly sobbed, claiming that Jeff's neglect had caused her to want to kill herself, Jeff felt chills running down his spine. He woke Molly's parents and then helped them to bundle Molly into the car to take her to the emergency room of the local medical center.

After Molly's wounds were treated, there was a psychiatric consultation in the early hours of the morning. Molly's parents blamed Jeff for what had happened to their daughter, and Jeff accepted responsibility, blaming himself for being "not good enough" to give Molly what she needed. After Molly was released, she and Jeff were forbidden to see each other, except at school. For Jeff, the end of the relationship was a huge relief. He didn't date again for six years.

When he was twenty, Jeff met Betty. He was immediately attracted to her, but there was a problem: Every time he tried to kiss and fondle her, he became panicked—an unusual and disturbing reaction in a strapping college sophomore. Troubled about himself, Jeff made his way to the student health clinic for some psychotherapy.

It didn't take long to figure out what triggered Jeff's panic attacks. Of course, his experience with Molly was shadowing his relationship with Betty. It may seem as if this should have been a no-brainer for him, but it wasn't. His fear of intimacy was unconscious. He'd been only fourteen when his relationship with Molly had ended so disastrously. His personality was not yet fully formed. Six years later, his self-blame, the nagging sense that "it was all my fault," had become buried although never erased. Now, sharing a simple kiss with a young woman who truly attracted him, in his mind, held the danger of beginning a scenario that would end in pain and anguish—and that would all be his fault.

Once Jeff recalled his experience with Molly, he was able to analyze and compare his relationship with her to that with Betty. He could now bring an adult rationality to the situation. Betty wasn't at all like Molly, he recognized: She was more mature, self-confident, trustworthy, and strong. Clearly, he had no need to fear that she was going to become fragile, needy, and overly dependent.

It took time, work, and new self-reflection for Jeff to move forward, but before the end of the semester, he was happily able to understand and thereby calm his reflexive anxiety, enabling him to deepen and enjoy his relationship with Betty.

CLARIFYING PERSONAL BOUNDARIES

For a relationship to work, each person must respect the boundaries of the other. Molly's extreme need for Jeff's attention brought her too close. He felt overwhelmed and suffocated by her overdependence. Many other people in unfulfilling relationships have sat in my office and complained that his or her partner was too remote. While intimate partners often do need "more space," they also need to declare and authentically show empathy, kindness, and connection. Beyond this need for occasionally living out and verbally declaring connections, intimacy requires that both people in a relationship establish spaces between them that are "just right," allowing each other solitude and separate outside pursuits whenever and to whatever degree is desired.

In adulthood relationships, boundaries protect intimacy. Every person needs respect; individual needs, feelings, attitudes, and values must be recognized and acknowledged. In a good partnership or marriage, much is shared—but not everything. Some couples preserve intimacy by agreeing to disagree on certain irreconcilable differences and respecting each other's privacy in that regard. Some couples maintain separate bank accounts, observe different religious practices, pursue different hobbies or social lives, and support different political parties. Friendly respect for individual roles and beliefs bridges differences and maintains closeness.

It stands to reason then that a violation of boundaries

is one of the surest ways to destroy intimacy. When a parent crosses the line with a child by being sexual, violent, or neglectful, the law recognizes such treatment as abuse and prosecutes the offenders. In adult interactions, violations may not be so clear. And some of us, for the sake of avoiding conflict, are too passive about clarifying, establishing, and defending the perimeters of our safe space. It helps to recognize the inner signals of a boundary violation, which often occur as a flare of tension, fear, or sense of backing off in response to a specific behavior on the part of the other person. These may be just flickers of minor distress, but they are worth considering as part of a repetitive pattern of discomfort that it is wise to recognize and clarify, at least in the privacy of one's own mind.

If you are in a troubled relationship and you want more intimacy, it may be quite helpful and worthwhile to take a careful look at how you and your partner have drawn your boundaries. Clarifying and tweaking your shared and separated spaces may help you create a closer connection. Remember, in establishing intimacy you are taking the other person as he or she is, not as your ideal or not as you hope to see your partner changed. This does not mean you cannot renegotiate terms within your relationship at any time; it is just that you do not have the right or ability to change another person's fundamental temperament, character, and values.

Issues about boundaries and attitudes toward intimacy often arise when circumstances change. As we enter new chapters in our lives, we can be presented with opportunities to confront and examine our old beliefs, to rewrite our mental map for relationships yet again. New parents, for example, are pretty sure to find that they aren't completely in sync about how to care for and raise their infant. These differences may be based on how they were raised and which of their own parents' attitudes they might want to avoid or emulate. How these disagreements are handled can enhance or ruin a relationship, as many couples have discovered.

Earlier negative experiences in relationships, whether they occurred when we were infants, children, and/ or adolescents, make us all vulnerable to engaging in unsatisfying and destructive patterns with everyone in our lives, especially with our own children, relatives, and friends, those to whom we're the closest. My message is that by recognizing this vulnerability and engaging in a little self-monitoring, you can plan and make appropriate adjustment in your behavior and thereby counteract your old, outmoded impulses. You can be a better parent than your mother or father may have been. You can be a better spouse or a better friend. Your values and judgments can evolve. You can replace an intuitive behavior with a new, conscious, moral principle, grow in maturity, and find your way to greater happiness.

BRIAN: GAINING A FRESH VIEW

Brian lived on a family farm in the rural Pacific Northwest until he went to the University of California at Berkeley, where he roomed with another freshman, Herb.

The two young men were in many of the same classes and soon were eating most of their meals together and going on weekend camping trips. They became almost insepa-rable... until one night Herb said that he had something to tell Brian. He wanted to be open about himself, about his sexuality. He was attracted to men, not women, he explained, but he also wanted to make it clear that he did not have any romantic feelings for Brian. He simply considered them great friends.

Brian was shocked and thrown into confusion. He'd never known anyone who was a self-identified homo-sexual. He had the notion that same-sex intimacy was a sinful, evil act and that people who engaged in it were disturbed. But Herb was a good person. Brian felt he knew him well, and terms such as *sinful* and *evil* or *disturbed* were in no way an accurate description of his friend.

Brian realized that his thoughts echoed the opinions of his parents, the pastor of his church, other members of the congregation, many of his school classmates. He'd been given the same message over and over through the years: Homosexuality was bad. No one had ever ques-tioned that assertion, and Brian couldn't imagine that so many of the people he'd always respected could be wrong. Therefore, his thinking went on, that must mean Herb's presentation of himself as a good person had been false; somehow Brian had been tricked into believing it. At the time and in his shocked state of mind, this was the only view that made sense, and Brian felt compelled to request a change in roommate.

Weeks later, however, he was still struggling with the

issue. Rather than feeling resolved, confident that he'd acted with conviction, true to his conscience, he felt a nagging sense of guilt and shame. He knew that he'd hurt his friend badly. His thoughts kept returning to the idea that Herb had worn a mask of goodness the entire time they'd known each other, a conclusion that just didn't hold up. In fact, Herb had never been dishonest, Brian was sure. Rather, Herb had been remarkably open and comfortable enough in their friendship to trust Brian with very personal information. Through this process of rational reappraisal, Brian revised his beliefs and attitudes. He still hadn't formulated any definitive ideas about homosexuality; that process would take more time. For now, it was enough that, based on his own reasoning, he was certain that whatever someone's gender preference might be, it was not a measure of character. Herb, an obviously good man in every way, was proof of that.

With honesty and integrity, Brian approached Herb with an apology and an explanation, knowing he was doing the right thing, and Herb accepted the gesture with gracious understanding. The friendship between the two young men was restored, even strengthened, as Brian took a leap of growth in maturity and gained a greater sense of peace with himself.

MACKENZIE: LONELINESS AND A MIDLIFE NEED FOR CONNECTION

Sometimes ingrained attitudes remain with us well into adulthood. Brian was a college freshman when he seized his opportunity to reassess his views, but Mackenzie was a successful forty-year-old businessman who was suffering from a loneliness that was caused by old, unconscious, fixed responses and that extended as far back as he could remember.

Mac had good relationships in the workplace, and he was also able to enjoy occasionally spending time with a few friendly acquaintances and former schoolmates. But he had no close friend or confidant and no committed romantic partner. In terms of intimate relationships, he felt a deep yearning.

He'd dated several women over the years, but these affairs had never lasted long. They'd ended with him feeling dissatisfied, bored, and critical of each woman's qualities and characteristics. The older he became the greater was his loneliness. He thought owning a dog might fill some of his need for companionship, but he was disappointed in how that had worked out, as well. For some reason, he felt remote even from Amber, his golden retriever.

In our early sessions together, I learned about Mac's childhood. His father had been mostly harsh and judgmental. His mother was often remote, seemingly overwhelmed by coping with her household of four children and perhaps periodically depressed. Mac's parents' marriage had not contained much joy either. Mac's father had called his wife "Mrs. Morose," which she'd seemed to accept with helpless remorse. Mac, too, had been criticized for being glum. His father had labeled him "Mr. Morose," and Mac often seemed to disappoint his father in other ways. Mac acknowledged that this was partly why he'd felt lonely for such a long time.

From the beginning, loneliness was the focus of Mac's therapy. In our first sessions, we explored his tendency to feel depressed and his difficulties connecting to others. I thought we were moving along quite well, but Mac's experience was different. My questions irritated him, he soon revealed. He felt I was being scornful, judgmental, critical, and disapproving of him in some covert way.

"It's good you're telling me this," I said. "Now I can reassure you that I'm not criticizing you at all. I'm merely looking for clarification, trying to understand your interpretation of what we're discussing. But your feeling of being judged tells me that what's happening here is what's known as 'father transference.' Your irritation with me is really anger at your father that you've previously suppressed."

Instead of considering this idea and processing the information, Mac got angrier. Now he felt that I was criticizing him for developing an inappropriate transference, for not working on *that*, and for not being more frank about his feelings about his father. Mac's expectation of criticism was so strong that he couldn't hear anything else.

Clearly, a nerve had been exposed, but it also presented an opportunity for understanding and healing. I pointed out to Mac how very sensitive he was to criticism and asked him to tell me whenever he felt that a judgmental attitude lurked behind my remarks or even if he suspected that I was having unspoken negative thoughts about him. Whenever he raised the point, we were going to consider if some of this criticism and disappointment might not, in fact, be arising from aspects of his own personality. (We were working on exposing old thinking as well as on integration on a route somewhat different from than that discussed in Lesson 3.)

In a later session, I wondered aloud if, once Mac had established a healthy, sexual relationship with a woman, he would anticipate the romance falling short? Did he have some standard he expected a relationship to measure up to? Did he perhaps end his affairs quickly to avoid the future disappointment that he somehow felt was inevitable?

The answers to these questions surprised—and shamed Mac. Yes, he did have a dreamy ideal relationship in his mind, and his actual experiences with women had never measured up to it. Asked for details, he described a very unrealistic adolescent concept of perfection in intimacy, perfection he had never witnessed in any real relationship. He felt very embarrassed to be over forty and still harboring such notions.

He was far from alone in reaching his fourth decade while still clinging to an adolescent fantasy, I assured him. The acquisition of self-knowledge is the work of a lifetime, and uncomfortable truths may emerge at any age. Tolerating those difficult feelings is how we acquire maturity and wisdom, and how we earn legitimate pride in having made the journey.

Once Mac became aware of his unconscious, unattainable ideal, he was able to reject it. He knew that any relationship would have little strains and problems, and he began paying much more attention to other moments of discomfort with the woman he'd recently begun dating. He realized that whenever she expressed a wish or a minor frustration about anything, Mac felt disappointment and criticism "in the air." To him, her unfulfilled desire instantly meant she was unhappy with their relationship, with him. When his girlfriend expressed an unmet need, Mac blew it into catastrophic proportions. He perceived her expressions of a desire or dissatisfaction as huge expectations he could never fulfill.

Mac had lived a lot of his life without being able to think or talk about wants, desires, and little frustrations. So I suggested that we practice changing that, unsettling the fixed attitude by using a language about needs. I began to make statements such as "I need to hear more about how you are feeling," "I want to know more about how you feel when you leave the session with me," "I need to know about how you feel before you ring the doorbell to my office."

This deliberate use of the words *need* and *want* made Mac laugh, but it also showed him that these words were not threatening. Hearing them didn't mean that he would be engulfed by neediness or that he was being accused and criticized of "not measuring up." The words didn't need to trigger anxiety within him and compel him to run for his life from the growing attachment of a relationship. This approach freed him to listen to someone articulate a desire without feeling overwhelmed by it, and it also helped him to see that he could express his own wishes without fear of rejection or censure. He developed in his own mind a language to identify and convey what he was feeling, and he came to understand for the first time the process of compromises and negotiations that occur in healthy, intimate, long-term relationships. He learned the concept of continuity: He might need to ride out rough patches in any connection with another—there are times when any two people will be out of harmony—but that was the nature of commitment, and now he understood that. His previous mental map of relationships had been distorted by expectations of disappointment and criticism. His new model was one of being close, mutually supportive, and able to accept the ups and downs

When Mackenzie left his therapy with me, he and his girlfriend were taking the next step in their relationship: making arrangements to live together. They were planning to rent a house in a pretty wooded suburb where Amber—whose needs no longer overwhelmed Mac—could get plenty of exercise on long walks with her owner.

ROLE-RELATIONSHIP MODELS

We all have inner models for relationships. As children, we first imitated behaviors, perhaps scolding our dolls and pets in the same manner we were reprimanded, or treating a playmate or stuffed toy sweetly or unkindly, depending on our experience with a sibling

As previously mentioned, each of us reaches adulthood having already developed a view of our self and of others, copying both an identity and a way of interrelating based on our observations and/or participation in exchanges with the people around us in the real world—at home, at school, and on the playground—as well as in fictional ones—on TV, at the movies, and in books. The sitcom characters and comic-book superheroes we loved may have influenced us more than we realize. The scenarios of our experience gave us expectations about relationships. We developed pretty good ideas about the responses and reactions that certain emotions were likely to trigger. Anger at home meant yelling, perhaps, or sadness made Mommy anxious, or asking for attention made Daddy grouchy, or, as Mackenzie experienced, the expression of a desire produced criticism and disapproval.

We each have a repertoire of behavior patterns to pull out as needed. The appropriateness of our responses and reactions to any given situation is a question of how rationally our early road maps were drawn or how well we may have revised them through the years. When we meet someone new, the first moments of encounter are full of potential to activate our established relationship models. The connection we make is colored by our state of mind. Our reading of the first signals, both verbal and nonverbal, is what accounts for attraction or repulsion, interest or disinterest. The ensuing signals fuel the evolving connection. It's not difficult to recycle an old transactional pattern. Each of us, of course, enters a relationship with a slightly different inner model. So, in fact, each of us has a different interpretation of what is actually happening. It is wise for all of us to keep that in mind, especially when the inevitable disharmony arises and our patterns for handling conflict may not be at all compatible.

When the little spats, moments of irritation, or blazing, out-of-control, flaming rows that occur in a relationship are all opportunities for growth, although they're rarely welcomed in such moments. We tend to overlook the chance for rational analysis and emotional growth in the heat of a battle; so we often remain stuck in old ruts and continue to have the same knee-jerk responses to the same stimuli decade after decade. Triggered by the old familiar circumstances, we lose our cool, lash out, tune out, become incensed, throw a tantrum, or treat our children in ways we once swore we never would.

When a partner sometimes says "Hey, you are treating me like your mother, and I am not like her," that observation may, in fact, be right-on. In psychotherapy the excessive use of inappropriate role-relationship models is called "transference." The development of a new, appropriate role-relationship model is called a "corrective relational experience." Brian had a corrective experience when he jettisoned the distorted views of homosexuality he'd learned from his parents and his hometown community and developed his own. Mac experienced transference when he heard disapproval and scorn in my probing questions, which also led him, in a reversal of roles, to be very critical of me. He had a corrective experience when I remained calm, nonjudgmental, and patient while I pointed out his irrational expectations and responses.

You can be your own therapist in this way. With attention, effort, and awareness, you can determine whether any relationship model activated in your mind really applies to a current relationship. The work can be slow, but you can improve on old patterns and have a corrective experience in any relationship if you give yourself the chance. A diary or a journal may be very useful in helping you achieve clarity. You probably already have a good idea of what pushes your buttons. A written review of events as they happen and a record of how you're reacting can help you develop a deeper understanding of those old impulses and thereby diminish their power.

It also helps to consider the needs, desires, wishes, and fears of others. Try to identify your intentions and motives. Consider whether or not you're projecting them inappropriately onto someone else. It's a struggle to correct our inner models so that they are appropriate. With honest self-observation and appraisal, you can develop a new view.

ATTITUDES

Attitudes comprise a mixture of thoughts, emotions, and responses that often stem from childhood and can last a lifetime... if a conscious effort isn't made to change them. Whether based on reality or misconceptions, attitudes can become thoroughly familiar, extremely repetitious, and deeply ingrained. When old attitudes are activated and projected into new relationships and current situations, they can disrupt, impede, and even poison intimacy.

Chronic resentment toward a parent for past abuse or neglect is common. Since no parent is perfect, many of us grow up experiencing some real distress and familial dysfunction. As small children, we see adults as powerfully good or bad. Parents might appear to be a beautiful fairy king and queen or an ugly ogre or evil witch. When we're little we also see ourselves at the center of the universe, which often leads us to believe that we have power over everything that happens and to take responsibility for the actions, moods, and even the health of those around us. This mind-set creates a pretty distorted lens for viewing what's really going on in our homes. Yes, Mommy and Daddy might have been self-absorbed sometimes, drunk sometimes, depressed sometimes, and tense and frustrated sometimes, but they may not have been nearly as malevolent as we recall; and our little childhood selves may be much less culpable for their moods and behaviors than the degree of self-blame and shame that may remain in our minds for many years.

As children, we simply don't have the capacity to understand all the factors of cause and effect. Yet in our immature mind using our magical thinking we create an enduring role-relationship model that we can later activate and misapply to adult relationships. Of course, some parents do batter, exploit, neglect, and abuse their children, but even in such cases, any use of an old role-relationship model in the present is still a misapplication.

Childhood abuse, real or imagined, often generates a persistent negative attitude and a tendency toward explosive mood swings. When we continue to carry into adulthood the wounds from the injustices we suffered as children, we take on the role of grievances collector to justify our bitterness. When we view ourselves as "wronged," we then see others as "victimizers." In this way, we carry on the past, projecting it inappropriately in the present. Aimed at a spouse or lover, this distorted perception can become a self-fulfilling prophecy, provoking the accused partner into responding with hot anger that echoes previous abusive behavior.

A role-relationship model that reflects abuse can contain three positions: victim, aggressor, and heroic rescuer. For an abuse survivor, all three roles can be present in the internal scenario, and the self can vacillate among them. At times, the self may reexperience the humiliation of victimization. In some primitive way, an abused child who accepts blame can still carry that shame as an adult. Alternatively, the adult may still harbor the child's view that an evil monster was responsible for the abuse, in which case he or she can take on the powerful role of aggressor, one who fights back and gets revenge. Then there is the role of protective champion who slays the villain, saves the day, and restores fairness and justice. It is this shifting between roles that accounts for the tendency of battered children to become battering parents, and it explains why so often they also are drawn to professions that involve protecting the innocent, such as social worker, police officer, or firefighter. They have learned to take on the corrective, stronger role.

Dark, unattractive moods and lightning-quick mood

swings are certainly impediments to intimacy. When memories and fantasies of childhood grievances are awakened by some frustrating event or when an old role model is unconsciously activated by a new argument, the harmony of a relationship can be devastated. But when childhood ideas are brought to the light of consciousness and are verbalized, primitive childlife thinking can quickly give way to the clarity of adult reflection. Lucid contemplation can overcome magical beliefs. The vicious cycle of intense emotions can be tamed into much more positive and situation-appropriate responses.

If you're aware that you have exaggerated responses to events (i.e., you fly into a rage if your housebroken dog has an accident on the rug; or you know the cashier who miscalculated your change is a thief out to fleece you for everything you've got), you can presume that you are in need of some attitude adjustments. Once you acknowledge and accept it, the solution to freeing yourself from that old baggage is within your reach, closer than you might imagine. Simple reasoning with yourself when severe inner turbulence erupts can help curb your tendency to inflate the seriousness of situations. As an adult, you have the wisdom of maturity on your side and the ability to bring humor into the equation. The dog with an urgency to urinate is not a demon out to get you, and you know it. The clerk who can't count coins is probably just another poor, distracted, sleep-deprived bloke who only wants to move you through his line and out the door.

Self-talk is a simple and extremely effective means of counteracting old beliefs and negative attitudes. For example, you might tell yourself: *As a child I may have believed I caused myself to be beaten because I was bad, but that was an error. I was not better or worse than any other rambunctious kid, and the fault was not mine. Back then, my father was rationalizing away his own regrets for his bad actions and loss of self-control by saying I caused all my own misery and his. I do not have to carry his rationalizations or anything else from that situation into my current life.*

The lesson is this: When a repetitive, irrational idea arises from circumstances within a close relationship, acknowledge it, take time to verbally clarify it, and then form a clear, more realistic, corrective attitude to counteract it. This may not be so easy to do, but it is important to stick with it. It's the hard work of change that can be deeply rewarding. You may need a thousand repetitions of the corrective attitude if you're already suffered a thousand repetitions of the dysfunctional one. The repetition of your new alternative attitude works slowly, but in time it can reduce the suffering caused by ingrained negative attitudes.

While you're working on improving your "erroneous" attitudes, you might find it beneficial to share your efforts with a trusted significant other. Chances are the people close to you, who are already familiar with your moods and hot buttons, can offer better perspective and help as you work to counter old ideas with corrective attitudes. Letting someone in on your attempts to alter your point of view and improve yourself can lead to a close connection and an enduring attachment between the two of you.

The benefit of "sharing" is not, however, a truism; sometimes your innermost struggles are best kept private. It's your choice. Whether you confide in another or not, the work will bear the fruits of bringing more integration in self-understanding and increasing the chances for deeper intimacy in your life.

❧ Teaching Points ❧

- People vary in their capacity for intimacy. Some of this variation is due to endowment, some to life experiences. In general, early traumas may make it harder to develop deep and constant affiliations later in life, but mastery of stress and later good experiences can ameliorate fears that traumas will be repeated.
- Learning from new opportunities, which can be enhanced by taking time to be explicit about erroneous expectations, almost always helps to increase happiness by increasing one's own capacity for intimacy.
- Learning from new opportunities is often called insight, which has three important characteristics:
  1. Understanding occurs more frequently the more you reflect upon how your own mind works: how you think, feel, and decide what to do next.

2. Insight is the monumental *aha* experience of understanding that can be positive and encouraging even if the memory that led you to it is unpleasant.

3. Insight is a body of knowledge that continually improves intimacy as you understand yourself and your intimate others more and more.

- Insight is a form of self-talking. That is, you hear yourself thinking, you see repetitive but perhaps inappropriate patterns, and voice within yourself your new and growing insightful correctives. This positive self-talking is more adaptive than repeating negative self-talking as in "Gee, I'm so stupid!" or "Things will never get better!"

- Remember that when you take the time necessary to review and revise your attitudes, you are not only learning mature views but also building your strength by learning how to learn and develop the skills involved in hatching insights.

Overcoming Grievances

Ongoing resentments can poison intimacy in all our close connections, but letting go of grudges and thoughts of revenge leads to freedom, better relationships, and greater happiness.

The First Wives Club, a best-selling book and popular movie, is a comedy about three divorcées who join forces to get even with the ex-husbands who betrayed them. The success of this plot with audiences doesn't surprise me. Revenge plots of all kinds—funny, dramatic, and deadly—have always been popular in the theater, movies, books, soap operas, and country and western songs. Hanging on to grievances and fantasizing about settling the score are common human experiences. Audiences identify with the victim and cheer when the villain is dealt a comeuppance. Fictional revenge is one way to reduce the painful gravity of the sadness, anger, and fears that are the residue of real betrayals.

Almost all of us have felt the sting of someone

"sticking it to us," then most likely replayed the hurtful incident mentally, over and over again, nursing the grudge. We human beings tend to do that: blame someone and then heap on more blame than is really justified. But imagining retaliation isn't in our own best interests; it's a threat to intimacy that must be acknowledged as such and counteracted.

Grievances can function as a kind of fuel: A good hostile revenge fantasy can be very effective in restoring a sense of powerfulness and overcoming feelings of vulnerability. Some of us feel better and vibrantly alive when we're fuming self-righteously. But plotting revenge or dreaming up retaliations never resolves problems or changes the person who has hurt us; it only undermines our own happiness and our ability to create new opportunities for intimacy. Getting out of the self-righteous zone is the true path to real self-empowerment.

Think about the costs of holding on to resentment: isolation, suspicion, vindictiveness, and more interest in reprisal than in the restoration of our own equilibrium. And the people we resent can take up residence in our minds, hanging around, influencing our behaviors, sometimes for years, even after being long gone from our actual lives. This is especially true when we allow childhood grievances to take up residence in our memory, coloring our adult responses and interactions. By nurturing resentments, we may be repeatedly re-creating scenarios in which we're victimized again, unconsciously making plans to change the outcome this time, to get even. We may also be caught in an unconscious pattern of role reversal, committing betrayals ourselves to avert feeling victimized anew. Such an attitude can keep us trapped in a mind-set that collects injustices, overreacts to perceived insults and injuries, and persists in seeking revenge.

Ideally, as we grow up and mature, we learn to attribute blame more fairly and tactfully and to apply understanding and forgiveness whenever possible. But like all of the work of happiness, it's an ongoing process. At any age it can be very wise to consciously consider if any of your childhood grievances are still active. You can look at how resentment has affected your happiness and then make a clear commitment to letting it go, even if you cannot reach a state of forgiveness. This may not always be easy, but just directing your attention toward your future and away from your past can be the start of feeling lighter and freer. You let go of a grievance, not to benefit anyone who has hurt you, but to unburden yourself, to lift your heart.

BERTHA: SHOOTING HERSELF IN THE FOOT

When we have been deeply wounded, the injury can provoke us into hurting ourselves further. Bertha's story is an example of this dynamic. When she was nine, a lonely child in a big, busy family, she was sexually fondled by one of her teachers. This trusted authority figure told her she was special and used her hunger for attention to manipulate her into being a willing participant in repeated violations throughout the school term. She wasn't this man's only victim; his pedophilia was eventually uncovered, and he disappeared from the school.

Bertha was left feeling terribly betrayed. Then, instead of receiving all the reassurance and guidance she needed, she was further wounded by other adults who conveyed the message that she had been a "dirty" child for having remained silent and having allowed the caresses to continue. Bertha took this unfair point of view to heart. In adolescence, living out the identity she'd been assigned and then adopted for herself, she became promiscuous. Later, she became a topless dancer and occasionally indulged in prostitution.

Eventually therapy helped her to overcome her sense of herself as a degraded woman and enabled her to reassess her history and acknowledge the injustices she had been subjected to. Of course, this wasn't an easy process; it progressed slowly, in phases. First, she had to remember the story of her past, which she had avoided thinking about for years, although its legacy had continued to influence her choices since childhood. When she began to let herself recall what had happened, she recognized how her perception of herself as "bad" and "dirty," a reflection of the attitudes of others, had been established. With a more accurate reappraisal of her memories, she was able to express her anger, both at the man who had violated her and at the other adults who'd responded inappropriately at the time, and to realize that she was harboring fantasies of revenge. They were dim and virtually unconscious yet still dynamically active, a subtle soundtrack running through her mind as she continued to engage in activities that made her feel debased. By working through these patterns and coming to understand herself, Bertha was able to make corrective choices and to let go of rage, self-disgust, self-accusation, and chronic bitterness.

Contemplation and maturity brought her a new more mature view of how she'd been caught in an ongoing cycle of abuse at the hands of a victimizer and of misguided outrage and ignorance on the part of the other adults who failed her at a critical time. With her past in perspective, Bertha was able to put to rest her passive submission to the idea that she was "bad" and to gain a sense of herself as a good woman with good connections to the world.

Bertha's history was terribly unfortunate but not uncommon. The degree of multigenerational abuse in our world has been slowly coming out of the closet over the last few decades. Consensus of how inappropriate it is to blame the victim has been growing. We've all become savvier about these issues and how to deal with them. As a culture we're recognizing how we have failed many of our children in the past. Bertha could take some comfort in knowing she wasn't alone in her experience.

Some crimes, however, are so egregious that feelings of betrayal and anger are hard to overcome. Rage and retaliation seem justifiable in the face of viciousness, callousness, and excessively cruel self-centered acts. Revenge, however, even in these cases, is never a good solution.

ACCEPTING THE UNACCEPTABLE

Imagine being exploited by someone you trust. Your best friend and your wife run off together. Your business partner embezzles all of your company's assets. Your lover infects you with the HIV virus by refusing to wear a condom, knowing the risk. Imagine losing a loved one because of someone's negligence: a drunk driver kills your child, or a neighbor in your apartment building falls asleep while smoking in bed and causes a fire that takes your pets and everything you own. These are just a few examples of some of the worst betrayals and losses that a person can suffer and some of the most difficult challenges to finding freedom from consuming rage. You've played no role in what has happened. Your world is completely devastated. In some cases, someone you loved may now be someone you hate.

Of course, you'd be traumatized, ablaze with anger, and consumed by a thirst for retribution. Yet, for your own sake, you would need to think your way through your grievance to actually let go and move on. There are many books and movies about just that: individuals who have found a way to transcend pain and rage and thereby free their heart and mind. This is a very emotional process that requires courage, character, maturity, and wisdom. If you've had this type of fiery experience and you can emerge from it whole, you will have found your way through a pivotal process of *A Course in Happiness*.

Fortunately, most of the grievances that occur in our day-to-day lives are not so catastrophic. We get angry with our colleagues, friends, relatives, and romantic partners over smaller transgressions: a breach of trust, an inconsideration, a violation of a boundary, or perhaps just plain repeated annoying behaviors that push our buttons. We vacillate between warm loving moments and episodes of irritation, exasperation, bickering, and sometimes loud, heated battles, but we know the conflict will pass. Eventually we'll regains our equilibrium; we won't hold on to hatred or remain in chronic emotional pain from our injury. We are much more likely to pardon a friend, coworker, or lover than we are a rapist, murderer, or deceitful manipulator. Still, it is not easy to stop nursing a grudge, and, regardless of the seriousness of the wrong, the process is the same.

Rage arises from deep and primitive innersprings. Whenever we are deeply hurt, it is almost a biological imperative to respond with aggression, just as an animal will attack when cornered. When we are injured, we get angry. It is part of our nature, and the passionate emotions that emerge from this powerful response do not dissipate quickly or easily, but they can be channeled. We can use reason to identify them as destructive impulses and then make conscious choices to govern and work through them.

Sometimes we cave in to pain and feel weak and deflated, or we fill up with menacing self-righteousness from which to lash out, both of which are unhealthy and self-defeating responses. Sometimes we churn with a primitive sense of disgust and wrongness. We want to lash out as a way of externalizing that judgmental attitude. In these instances, too, the path to healing is through self-knowledge and conscious corrective choices.

Centuries of wisdom have recommended forgiveness. Religions around the world encourage it, and there is a plethora of adages that reminds us of the value in struggling through grievances, but as a clinician, I recognize forgiveness as a goal that cannot always be achieved. It is an ideal. Most of us do the best we can at letting go of anger and hurts, and, from my point of view, if we are making an effort to move on, we are on the right track.

True freedom from grievances requires first identifying, understanding, and then reorganizing the complexity of thoughts and emotions that arise within the inner turmoil of rage. The goal of this struggle is to find understanding between the extremes of pathological avoidance and blinding, ongoing, blazing hostility. Letting go and moving on does *not* mean refuting anger or lifting blame, nor does it mean avoiding the issue by setting it aside and choosing not to think about it. Meek submission will not help develop maturity. Letting go *does* mean refraining from stoking the fire of rage, for to remain stuck in fury is always detrimental. When we're consumed with thoughts about the past actions of someone who has harmed us, we remain in the role of victim, not acting in our own best interests for the future. But by working through wrath and then trying to let it go, repeating the process again and again, if necessary, we are mastering our own happiness, even if we cannot fully forgive.

Do not do onto others what you would not want them to do to you is a version of the Golden Rule that may be the most concise and best advice against revenge and brutality. Yet following such advice is not automatic, not until vengeful feelings and raw impulses are first understood and brought under control. Similarly, Buddha's counsel—Holding on to anger and seeking revenge against your enemy is like picking up a hot coal: Before you can throw it, you have burned yourself—is another good reminder. But just reflexively saying "I forgive thee" won't help you achieve true peace of mind and heart. Deep-seated grievances and cores of resentment cannot be diffused with an adage. In fact, speaking empty words of forgiveness can be a defense against actually confronting feelings. Genuine letting go and increased personal resilience can only be achieved by acknowledging pain, experiencing it, working through it, and then moving on.

Other sage advice that helps me stay alert to the pitfalls of nursing grievances includes: *When you feel bitter, seek the good.* I saw this adage on a bumper sticker, and it's excellent advice, for if we are busy looking for goodness in our wretchedness, we won't be so prone to sinking into self-defeat or to wanting to hurt others. *Do not pass hatred on, fight it with compassion. The best cure for an enraged heart is comforting others.* The New Testament tells us to *turn the other cheek.* The Old Testament speaks of *an eye for an eye, and a tooth for a tooth*, which I interpret as an admonition to respond appropriately to an inflicted injury. An injured victim should take a measured and reasoned course in retaliating, to take *only* an eye for an eye and a tooth for a tooth.

Inspiring stories of other people, mantras, adages, and religious teachings are all reminders and helpful aids to getting us past a grievance. Nonetheless, most of us have to work hard and with a steadfast commitment to struggle through our greatest challenges.

FLORA: WORKING THROUGH A SENSE OF UNACCEPTABLE BETRAYAL

Flora had been happily married to Albert, a photojournalist, for five years. The couple had a two-year-old daughter, Sarah, whom they adored. They felt ready for a second child and had just begun trying to conceive when Albert was assigned to work with a highly regarded reporter on international stories. He went with a news team to the Middle East to cover unfolding events in Afghanistan. The distance of thousands of miles and the intensity of the breaking stories meant that Albert's assignment was prolonged. It was three months before he returned home.

From the moment she saw him again, Flora thought Albert seemed changed, somewhat reticent and brooding. When they were finally alone together in their bedroom, embracing, resuming their sexual relations, Albert shocked Flora by insisting on wearing a condom. The mood vanished in an instant. She demanded an explanation. Albert admitted that he had gonorrhea, a sexually transmitted disease. He was at the tail end of taking antibiotics to cure it, but he still needed to take precautions against infecting her.

Flora was flabbergasted and deeply hurt. Albert had broken his vow to be faithful. It was a betrayal she'd never imagined. Albert said that he loved her and only her and that he had never done anything like this before, in spite of previous temptations and opportunities. He had been in a foreign city. He'd felt lonely and depressed. One night, he'd gone out with a group of correspondents and had had too much to drink. He had only a dim memory of having unprotected sex with a woman he'd met in the bar. He begged Flora for forgiveness, weeping with sincere remorse.

Flora could only speak angrily. She asked him to sleep on the couch. The next morning, she treated him with icy disdain, although there was a part of her that did not want to be so remote. Flora brooded for hours. While doing some housework, she came across his tennis racket and on sudden impulse picked it up, took it to the stove, and held it over the gas flame until the strings burned. As the acrid smell of molten plastic filled her nostrils, she had a spasm of self-disgust. *How childish of me! How could I have done this?* Her feelings alternated between fury at Albert and shame at herself. Overwhelmed by an emotional flood, she sobbed.

In the following days, Flora had unbidden images of Albert having sex with another woman. She could not rest. Her temper flared every few hours. She believed Albert's story, but infidelity and disease so seriously breached their deep commitment and holy love, she did not know how she could ever get past it. She was so distraught that she turned to counseling to help her sort out her thoughts and emotions.

In our first session, I asked her about her expectations of marriage. As with most of us, she had a long-standing fantasy about a perfect union. Before she'd even met Albert, she'd planned a courtship, a wedding, and a marriage based on mutual devotion. Flora and Albert's elaborate church ceremony and wedding banquet had helped her actualize part of this fantasy. She loved Albert for who he was, but she also loved him because she projected onto their intimacy a kind of Hallmark-greeting-card poetry of perfection. The reality of Albert's infidelity was so incongruent with her vision of how her marriage should be that she felt her heaven had been trampled upon and turned into a hell.

"What do you imagine could be the most ideal scenario to come out of this situation?" I asked Flora.

After some thought, she told me she would like to be able to think of Albert's infidelity as a one-time aberration; something that would never, ever happen again. He'd been drinking. He was tired, he was caught up by group contagion in the release from responsibility, and he'd been seduced. These factors were the culprits. Albert had had a single lapse because he was drunk and not responsible. She and he were—and always would be—the perfect couple. Surviving the incident would strengthen their union. She could forgive and forget all about it.

"And what do you imagine the most catastrophic outcome would be?" I wanted to know next.

"That Albert will go on and on being unfaithful," she said, fighting tears at the thought. "That I've been terribly wrong about him all along, that he's actually a secret womanizer, and that I'll have to end our marriage now rather than wait to endure further betrayals."

"Now try to consider what really happened, how it's changed you and your marriage, and how you can achieve an outcome that would most benefit your future," I suggested.

What really happened, she admitted, was that Albert had a sexual encounter that he probably would never have told her about it if he hadn't contracted gonorrhea. Yet his contrition was genuine. Her image of the perfect marriage was tarnished, but she still loved Albert, even if he was less than perfect. Their marriage was sound, and she wanted it to continue for Sarah, herself, and for Albert. And she still wanted another child.

This realistic line of thought steadied Flora. She felt calmer. She told me she would speak to Albert about forgiving him. She planned to talk to him calmly, to set in motion what she believed was a rational plan to resolve their problems.

But it wasn't so easy. Her thinking may have become more reasoned, but her feelings of rage and betrayal hadn't been subdued. She now wanted to forgive Albert, but her heart wasn't ready. She continued to ask him to sleep on the couch. When he was around, she found it hard to feel anything other than resentment. She had fantasies about flirting with the attractive manager at her grocery store or calling an old boyfriend to "get even." But she restrained herself. She realized that her preoccupation with revenge, while it felt at first like "being strong," would only harm her family further if she carried it out.

She struggled to get past her spasms of anger and constant coldness. She told Albert that she'd thrown away his tennis racket. Better that, than him, she said. Anyway, she was sorry and she would replace it. He seemed relieved and accepted her apology gallantly, but she refused his attempts to hug her, asking him to be patient with her.

In our sessions, Flora talked about how her belief in having a perfect marriage had been shattered. She spoke over and over about how her perceptions had changed and about her new reality. Gradually, this repetitive effort stilled her mind and calmed her fury. She was angry. She still resented the episode. But she was in control of herself and her actions. In other words, each time she thought through the matter, she put the bad incident into perspective with all her good memories and her future expectations for her marriage. Her empathy—for herself, Albert, and Sarah—grew.

But Flora had another hurdle to overcome. From the time she was a teenager, she knew that if she were ever betrayed she'd handle it absolutely differently from the way her mother did. Flora's father had been an excessive drinker given to violent rages. When he was drunk and out of control, Flora's mother would throw him out of the house. When he was sober, charming, and apologetic, she'd welcome him back. Flora saw the cycle. She tried telling her mother that her dad's abusive behavior was just going to recur, but her mother insisted each time that her husband was now just fine. Flora knew better. She recognized denial and rationalization when she heard it. She also saw her mother as an ineffectual woman who cast both herself and Flora in the role of victims.

Flora had always been determined to be different from her mother. She was also determined to have a marriage different from her parents'. In her immaturity, she thought she'd dodged that bullet by marrying the perfect man. Now she would not deny or disavow her husband's bad behavior, but that did not mean that the only choices were "stay" or "leave." Flora had to get past that kind of adolescent thinking as well. Albert wasn't her father. What had happened to her marriage wasn't a total catastrophe. With her eyes wide open, Flora could choose to resume closeness with her husband without reenacting her mother's pattern.

As she grappled with all this and sorted it out in her thinking, Flora was able to begin talking to Albert about her struggle to get over her rage. She told him that she wanted to forgive him and get back to their mutual love.

Albert said he understood, expressed more remorse, and reaffirmed his intention to be faithful. Flora once again began to feel warm toward him because he had received, understood, and responded to what she was saying. Their reconciliation didn't happen instantly, but it was underway. And Flora now knew that they weren't likely to live "happily ever after," that there would be ups and downs, but along with more maturity in her marriage and her thinking, she had also developed a much more effective program for handling herself and her possible future conflicts with Albert.

Exercise: Examining What Mars an Intimate Relationship

1. Begin with the present. List the pros and cons of your relationship. No intimate connection between two people is ever perfect. Beware of overemphasizing the good or the bad points, and try to avoid totalistic thinking, seeing your relationship as all good or all bad rather than recognizing that you and your partner each have desirable as well as undesirable traits that will be reflected in a more balanced view of your relationship. Be as honest and realistic as possible, and remember that some of the smallest kindnesses can be a very big "pro," while a very slight inconsideration needs to be counted as a "con."

2. Consider the past. Are some of the "cons" grievances you are carrying around when you might be better off letting them go? Are you unfairly displacing some grievance from the past—ongoing anger about how you were neglected or smothered by a parent perhaps—onto your current significant other? Are you exaggerating a current "con" because of an expectation based on a past experience that you will be harmed in some way?

3. Look to the future. Develop three images of where your intimate relationship is heading. Picture an idealized vision of the future relationship; a catastrophic vision; and the most realistic vision you can formulate. By first considering the two extremes, you may uncover some of your most irrational expectations and fears, ones you must abandon before you can arriving at a more balanced middle ground.

4. Be aware of the present moment. Is there some abiding resentment you can now tell yourself to "just let go"? If it returns, remind yourself to let it go as often as needed, and keep telling yourself to move forward rather than remain stuck in the past.

TRAPPED BY THE PAST

Revenge ideas are easy to sow and hard to give up. Listen to any talk-radio program, and you're sure to hear callers spewing venom full of rage and blame. Seething anger is energizing. Thoughts of retaliation fuel feelings of strength and competence, eclipsing any sense of frailty, emptiness, or apathy.

When we're immature, we see the world in black and white. We rate others as either totally trustworthy or totally untrustworthy. With maturity, we learn to see many shades of gray between these extremes. We know people sometimes make mistakes. We get better at reading others' intentions. We weigh the degree of selfishness and caring we see in another, and we learn when and how to protect ourselves from broken promises, deceptions, and other acts of treachery, that is, unless we get stuck in a state of indignation, trapped by a past injury or insult to the self.

Betrayals strike at the essence of who we are; they undermine our sense of worth. And since most of us feel some uncertainty about our own agendas, a betrayal strikes at the heart of our vulnerability. Therefore, understandably, it creates intense rage, sadness, and fear. Breaking free of such strong negative emotions is difficult.

Some people develop self-righteous traits after a betrayal. They go through life with a chip on their shoulder, expecting duplicity, disloyalty, or con artistry everywhere. Sometimes they need only a shred of a reason to become indignant, even misinterpreting kind gestures, proclaiming them inadequate, and continue raging as long as possible. These individuals hold a constant grievance against the world, an irrational attitude reinforced by every new betrayal. In some cases, the fear that no one can be trusted and the belief that the universe is malevolent lead to impulsive acts of hostility. Aggression can be displaced onto a weaker target, such as a dog or a child. Such venting, in turn, leads to shame and guilt. It's a terrible cycle.

Recurring thoughts about betrayal and a running inner monologue of anger increases bitterness and diminishes happiness. The only way out is through a kind of healing I call "working through to a point of some completion."

There are six steps in this process:

1. Facing the facts of what has happened as straight-forwardly as possible
2. Developing understanding about what has occurred through honest appraisal
3. Amending any incorrect beliefs or exaggerated interpretations
4. Considering new choices about how to respond
5. Planning new strategies and tactics to deal with the emotional fallout (negotiating these with others, if appropriate)
6. Acknowledging that the decision-making process has been completed and moving on, letting go of previous unrewarding preoccupations

Looking back and reviewing the memory of betrayal and the powerful emotions it evoked may be painful, but it's a necessary journey if you want regain feelings of competence and self-worth and to develop realistic and reasoned beliefs about trust. When we recognize the trap of indignation and step away from it, we can become strong without rages. We can analyze current situations without replaying an endless loop that gets us nowhere.

SUE: HOLDING ON TO HURT

"You can never trust anyone," Sue, a thirty-five-year-old graduate student told me the first time I met her. She'd entered therapy to consider why she was always having such difficulty maintaining an intimate and satisfying relationship.

The reason we uncovered stretched back to a time long before she'd ever gone on a date or thought about romance. She'd been four years old when she was sent to live with her mother's sister, Zelda, who was a young wife at the time with two children of her own, both still in diapers. From the moment of Sue's arrival, she felt like a burden. Over the years, she never got close to her aunt or to her cousins. Now, more than thirty years later, she still felt bitter toward her mother—and toward anyone else who let her down in the slightest way.

In our sessions, Sue reviewed memories of her feelings about her mother's betrayal. "She didn't want me around, interfering with her good time," she said, a pronouncement born of bitterness and anger that certainly did not convey the larger context. But Sue wasn't ready to see that yet.

When Sue was conceived, her mother, Liz, had been seventeen. She and Sue's father, also a teenager at the time, tried making a go of their little family, but they were unsuccessful. By the time Sue was four, Liz was an abandoned single mother. Unemployed, facing homelessness, she'd turned to her sister for help, and Zelda offered a safe haven for Liz's little girl.

Like all small children, Sue imagined that her mother was able to do anything and everything. When we are little, we all believe our parents to be omnipotent; they contain the world for us in our dependency. Sue saw her mother as selfishly refusing to be her mom. I gently asked Sue if she really thought her mother was having many good times. Considering this question was the beginning of her attempt to review the past from a truly adult perspective.

Rightfully or wrongfully, when a child experiences suffering, he or she is going to blame someone. It could be him- or herself, but it is often a parental figure. This is normal. Children are self-centered: They ignore any factors involved in the chain of events that caused their suffering. From a child's point of view, any parental lapse is regarded as if it were purposeful, no matter what the reason. In adolescence, this blame turns to contempt. In adulthood, the truth of parental limitations can be realized, but this is not necessarily automatic or easy if one has become bitter along the way. Every new frustration fuels this poisonous attitude, intensifies the insatiable quest for compensation that others are seldom likely to provide, and provokes bursts of raw rage when needs are not met.

In therapy, Sue quickly recognized the childishness of her belief in her mother's omnipotence, which softened her sense of having experienced a traumatic betrayal. She also saw how she fueled her own bitterness by assuming that every new person in her life would soon reject her for selfish reasons. Of course, everyone at some time acts in some way or displays some trait that could be considered "totally selfish." Breakups happen, and sometimes for good reasons. The point, Sue realized, was that others balance their responses with issues of self-concern, and if she ever wanted to overcome some of her loneliness, risking connection would be necessary.

With this new consciousness, she was able to inhibit her tendency to collect injustices. She became aware of inner dialogues that suggested the world owed her restitution, and she revised them. Most significantly, she turned off the self-talk that predicted negative results when she got to know another person well.

Sue became a stronger person who was able to tolerate solitude, even though she still felt unsatisfied and alienated some of the time. The belief that it was better to be strong than weak was once the motivating force in her behavior with men. After the initial rush of mutual attraction, she would look for what she feared most: the signs of her date's potential disinterest. His glance over her shoulder at another woman might be all it would take for her to tell herself it was time to dump this man before she got dumped. She had to learn to check this automatic tendency, thwarting the self-fulfilling prophecy that prevented her from sustaining a long-term relationship. She became able to stick it out past the first romantic thrill and began dating men with a genuine interest in discovering who they were and how well her relationship with them might develop in genuine shared interests and affection.

Over the years, Sue had rebuffed all of her mother's efforts to get in touch, but eventually she reached the point of exploring the possibility of renewing that relationship, and the two women met several times. Their reunions were not filled with hugs and tears, the stuff of made-for-TV-movies, but Sue's understanding of her mother and of herself increased. Her heart was more at peace, and her future was filled with more positive possibilities.

MOVING ON

An unhappy childhood can never be erased. Like Sue, we can, upon adult reflection, develop more empathy for our parents and blame them less. This doesn't mean that our memories and attitudes will change to a happy view. In fact, when a life story is revised and realistically appraised, the reflections often lead to sadness, even a delayed mourning for childhood losses. If you white-knuckled it through all your growing-up years, living with family dysfunction, neglect, or abuse, you have good reason to grieve as an adult. Your childhood can never be relived with healthier or more nurturing parents. But making the passage through grief, as difficult as it may be, could be one of the most worthwhile journeys of your life. It is when you pass through the dark canyon of reviewing a distressing life story that you can let go of some its repetitive memories and expectations.

Through this inner work, you will be ready to seize the here and now and look to the near future for happiness. New, warm, loving relationships in various areas of your life will help you heal the wounds of childhood. You can forgive yourself for your prior resentments and make amends for acts of vindictiveness, if necessary. You weren't as much to blame when you were a child as you may once have thought. You may choose to break off completely from anyone with whom you can't reconcile. Or you may, like Sue, be able to renegotiate a relationship with individuals who once hurt you and who most likely wrestled with their own painful pasts and inner demons.

Practicing letting go of grievances does not mean condoning enduring wrongs; it simply takes the humanness of the offenders into consideration and discourages demonizing them. It's important to remember that letting go of vengeful feelings and bestowing absolution are not the same.

Episodes of severe betrayal and victimization, such as sexual violations, may never be forgotten, but the urge for revenge can still be held in check. The first task is to determine the right thing to do for justice and for your self-respect. For example, you may wish to involve the criminal justice system. Once you've taken action, it's time to move on, to let go of repetitive and intrusive memories, continued grievances and the urge for revenge.

Self-talk can turn the mind away from thoughts of retaliation, such as *There is that memory again, but I plan to move on with my life without reprisal.* Another technique that might help with moving on is to hold a one-sided conversation with the perpetrator or offender, denounce the wrongs that were committed, and then declare that no further punitive action is going to be taken. Some people do this by writing a letter, waiting, and then deciding whether or not to send it. Just writing it helps some, even if it is then tossed symbolically in the wastebasket. Like any therapeutic practice, this may not be the correct thing to do if it doesn't feel right. I mention it only as one means in which a memory of abuse may be put to rest.

BOB AND TED'S DISAPPOINTING VENTURE

Bob and Ted met in college, where they discovered they shared many idealistic values. They became best friends. After graduation, they decided to become business partners. It was their hope that they could reduce the discharge of toxins into sewers and waterways by establishing a nonprofit organization to recycle discarded solvents.

The two young men believed their plan could protect the environment and be applied everywhere, once they demonstrated its feasibility and effectiveness locally. Their strategy was first to identify the toxins, document a chemical process to decompose them, draw up a fiscally sound business plan to carry out the operations, and then apply for grants to supply their salaries. Until then, they would have to work many unpaid hours. In the interim, both men would need a paying job.

Ted found work at a coffee shop, and Bob entered the ground floor of a new business his father was developing, an outgrowth of his successful circle of enterprises. During the first month, when the two men had agreed to work out the details of their initial grant application, Bob's business required him to work long hours. Ted undertook most of the work alone.

The next month, Bob spent even more time immersed in his family's business, while Ted quit his coffee shop job to devote himself to a big push to finish the grant proposal. Two weeks later, when Bob still hadn't come through to work on the joint project, Ted reached the end of his rope. He felt that he was making all of the sacrifices and Bob had reneged on his pledge of partnership. When Ted confronted him with these accusations, Bob became angry and resigned from the project.

Ted felt totally betrayed. Hurt and angry, he told friends what Bob had done, damaging Bob's reputation in the process. The more Ted thought about Bob's defection the more he viewed his former friend as a callous, selfish adversary.

Ted decided to seek counseling to help him through this firestorm of emotion. "I hope his family business goes bankrupt!" Ted told me in our first session. One night, after drinking too much, he called Bob and told him the same thing he had told me. Afterward, he was filled with remorse and shame.

Ted was a religious young man. He believed in the teachings of his church. He felt he "should" forgive Bob, but his vengeful thoughts raged on, despite the commands he was giving himself to "let it go." He tried using self-talk techniques. He repeatedly said to me, "I forgive Bob," but his affirmations didn't arrest his daydreams about revenge. He continued to have hostile fantasies.

Then we tried the three-scenario technique in our sessions. I asked Ted to put the worst possible spin he could on the situation. "Bob was leading me along," Ted said. "He encouraged me to take a low-paying job, while he'd be making a lot of money working for his dad, thereby winning some kind of competition with me." In this unreasonably suspicious appraisal, Ted said, "I can see Bob gloating over my being trapped in the stupidity of my high ideals" and smiled ruefully. It was a ludicrous train of thought, of course; Bob was never as brutal or vain as Ted had been depicting him.

Next, Ted envisioned the opposite possibility, a scenario in which Bob totally capitulated, displaying once again his selflessness and idealism. "He'll come to me with a sincere apology, looking for a way to make up for what he's done," Ted said. "He'll devote a generous part of his income to the project. Perhaps his family business will endow a philanthropic grant to fund it!" He gave a laugh at the grandiosity of the outcome he'd imagined.

Thinking about these two extremes and the implausibility of them helped Ted clarify his thinking and arrive at a much more balanced view. Realistically, Bob might no longer be as idealistic as he had been in college, but he was still a good person. "Bob backed out of our agreement, but I knew he felt bad later," Ted said. As a young adult, Bob had become more pragmatic, appreciative of the rewards of working in a family business. Ted could see the advantage of that, too. The lucrative income would increase the quality of Bob's life; he would have the wherewithal to be of service in other meaningful ways.

Ted began to consider that Bob might never have been the perfect ally that he'd idealistically imagined and that perhaps he himself had never been perfect either. He'd wanted Bob to stay involved with the project, regardless of his perilous finances or career consequences. Maybe it hadn't mattered enough to Ted that Bob might have been letting his family down if he'd given the nonprofit project priority, as Ted had wanted.

This thinking led Ted to relinquish some of his hostility, to begin to forgive Bob, and to detach himself from the belief that Bob had been his best, truest, and most perfect friend. He could give up the deep affiliation he'd felt for Bob and let go of his revenge fantasies, although he did have to mourn the loss of his adolescent ideal of having a brother-like partner to promote his values and his enterprise.

Ted was able to replace his idealized self-image (*I would never betray anyone or be selfish*) as well as the devalued one (*I am going to look out only for myself from now on, just like Ted*) with a more realistic view of himself: *I might be self-serving in some circumstances*. By undertaking this important emotional work, Ted had avoided the pitfall of never trusting anyone again, lest he feel let down. Now he could ask himself who he could trust and then make a good decision based on his answer to that question.

WATCHING YOUR BACK

The act of letting go is a worthy goal, but in some cases being totally forgiving and turning the other cheek can mean setting yourself up to get slapped again. The type of realistic thinking that I want to encourage is as much about self-protection and realistic responses as it is about freedom from the desire for revenge.

After a betrayal, it is appropriate to take a hard look at the individual who has harmed you to determine how selfish and deceitful his or her motives and actions were. If you have been let down by someone who is totally selfish but who then wants to charm his or her way back into your good graces, it is in your own best interest to break off the relationship. When Bob made his agreement with Ted, he had been authentic in his desire to form an alliance with Ted and not deceitful or subversive. He believed in the commitment he was making *at the time*. He hadn't set out to pose, lie, or deliberately trick Ted. He also had the competence to fulfill his pledge; he just didn't turn out to be reliable in keeping it. Consequently, it might be reasonable for Ted to repair his relationship with Bob, to resume some aspects of the friendship, albeit with some revised expectations regarding Bob's reliability or lack thereof regarding future agreements. On the other hand, were Ted to realistically appraise Bob as being not only unreliable but also inauthentic, or as incompetent to fulfill an offer, then he might not want to repair the relationship.

Rational appraisal means being prepared, adequately defended, and continually alert to danger while rejecting the negativity of unending battles and vendettas.

☀ Teaching Points ☀

- Look out for any persistent grievances that you may be harboring. A betrayal is shocking and anger justified, but protracted revenge fantasies make matters worse. Revenge feels strong, but resisting it is where real strength lies.

- Consider if you have a chip on your shoulder. Avoid projecting your bitterness inappropriately onto others. Contemplation and empathy for both yourself and others can soften bitterness and increase compassion.
- Three-step thinking can help you soothe an angry heart: Put an idealized spin on the situation, imagine a catastrophic scenario, and then consider the most realistic appraisal. The resulting clarifications may lead to more rational thinking, thereby increasing the appropriateness of your future choices.

PART THREE

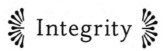 Integrity

Setting the Heart Straight

People's better angels are their conscious values.

Almost every day, I cross the Golden Gate Bridge twice, and I always marvel at what a feat of engineering it is, combining exquisite loveliness with essential function. Spanning the rough waters at the opening of San Francisco Bay into the Pacific Ocean, this graceful single suspension bridge provides a vital link between the city of San Francisco and Marin County. The cables, towers, and roadbed sway and give way under the stress of high winds, yet the structure is totally trustworthy while it eloquently speaks to the human longing for beauty. It is one of my favorite objects of integrity.

Like the Golden Gate Bridge, we gain integrity when we are able to integrate our needs, desires, and values. When we align what we think, say, and do; when we are honest, sincere, loyal, ethical, fair, just, honorable, and respectful, we are acting with integrity. Of course, we're all subject to many conflicting desires, commitments, and values that shift and change over time. Almost

everyone feels the pull of competing desires and obligations sometimes. But when we know ourselves well and
can reconcile our self-interests and our desire for social
connection with our moral obligations to others, we
increase our capacity for intimacy, our self-esteem, and
our happiness.

Soon after we're born we begin to learn morality, ethics, and a sense of justice, which dominate our thinking
throughout much of our lives. As toddlers we get our lessons from cartoons, TV programs, fairytales, movies, and
picture books. Throughout our childhood and adolescence, parents, preachers, teachers, coaches, scout leaders,
and numerous other mentors repeat these messages loud
and clear. Issues of right and wrong and admonishments
about what we "should" or "should not" do appear in
every type of print media, resound every Sabbath from
pulpits of every faith, and supply radio and TV talk show
hosts with seemingly endless topics for discussion. Different authorities have very different ideas about which
values are paramount, so it's no wonder we develop conflicts within our own minds about our own priorities.

In therapy, patients often talk about the "committee"
in their head, the voices that weigh in, argue, and advo-
cate for one moral position or another. It's our nature to
have an intuitive sense of goodness, but it's also natural
for us to want good things for ourselves. At times these
two inclinations are not aligned. It's easy to know what is
bad and what is good. It's much more difficult to choose
between two goods. Ending the argument, establish-

ing priorities, and reaching a reasoned decision that says what comes first takes effort, self-examination, sorting, and often reprioritizing. It's important, worthwhile work that goes hand in hand with the first two pillars of happiness: integration and intimacy. When we work on our integrity, we reap the benefit of less discord within our own mind, earn greater genuine respect from others, and improve our ability to maintain intimacy in our close relationships.

FIRST LESSONS IN SORTING VALUES

Integrity begins in childhood, of course, in unsteady little baby steps, like all the other important character developments that are at the foundation of true emotional and psychological maturity. If we're lucky, we get good guidance in figuring out how to manage the conflicts, ambiguities, and dilemmas of prioritizing wishes and principles. If we're not so lucky, if the adults around us floundered with their own ethics and failed to provide us with a shining example of honorable behavior, it's never too late to reexamine and reconcile our values, choices, and behaviors.

The first struggle I remember with the inner push/pull of conflicting values occurred when I was about seven. My mother had established geographic boundaries for me around our apartment building beyond which I was sternly ordered not to wander. I liked being a good boy and obeying my mother, but I also longed for adventure. The area around our building was familiar and boring to me, and I was occasionally tempted to explore further than I was allowed to. When I returned home, my mother would ask me where I'd been, and I wasn't above fibbing, telling her that I'd remained within her assigned perimeters. I wanted to satisfy my need for exciting activity, and, in some dim way, I wanted to resist her total control over me too. Even at that young age, I had a sense that it was good to avoid blind obedience to authority.

"I can tell when you're not being honest," my mother would say. "If you don't tell the truth, your nose will grow like Pinocchio's."

She was trying to help me develop a conscience, and her scolding did cause me concern about my deceit. I half-believed her prediction, although I suspected it was irrational. I liked the pictures in the book about Pinocchio, and I identified with the wooden puppet that broke a few rules to have fun, so I worried my nose just might grow like his if I didn't always tell the truth.

Intuitively, I knew my mother's rules were designed to keep me safe and I was wrong to disobey her. Thinking about it, I could reason that I was just a kid, not as competent as an adult, and that there was likely more danger in the world than I could have known. In other words, I came to realize that my mother's boundaries were not intrusive curtailments of my fun but reasonable restrictions for my protection. This thinking increased my inner harmony. I came to a self-owned principle about my relationship to rules that enabled me to manage my urge for the excitement of exploring. I developed self-governing principles. In time, I also learned to negotiate rules with my mother and then follow through on our agreements, which further increased my evolving integrity.

All children struggle with these sorts of dilemmas. That's why a story such as Pinocchio and a hero such as Spider Man remain popular with every generation. Finding the balance between stretching the rules and still remaining "good" is an important passage on the road to growing up. As children mature, the issues become more complex; reasoning and value systems evolve.

In *The Adventures of Huckleberry Finn,* Mark Twain tells a tale about developing integrity in a straight, clear series of events, actions, and consequences. Seeking adventure, Huck Finn sets out from home against parental approval to discover the world. At first, he's a detached observer, witnessing the misery of slavery, but then Huck begins to empathize with the slaves and feel an impulse to right the wrongs perpetrated by the strong against the weak. Thus motivated, when Tom Sawyer appears on the scene, both Huck and Tom risk their own safety to rescue an escaped slave and are rewarded with an increase in self-esteem and with a higher quotient of integrity.

Sometimes real life works the same way, but sometimes the course of developing integrity is a bit more complicated. As such, it can be helped or hindered by parents and other adults who may or may not understand a situation or offer appropriate responses.

BRIAN: CAUGHT IN A MORAL DILEMMA

Eight-year-old Brian was left at home to watch over his five-year-old sister while their mother made a very quick run to pick up their father at the train station. Just moments after she left, Brian's sister ran across the living room, fell, and cut her forehead on the sharp edge of a table. It wasn't a severe injury, but it bled a lot. Brian knew the right thing to do was to wash it and then cover it with a Band-Aid. But the Band-Aids were in the medicine cabinet, which he could reach only by standing on a stool, and both children had been told repeatedly that they were never to go into that cabinet.

Brian's sister was crying, her wound was red, and when he rinsed off the cut and saw the bleeding trickle to a stop, Brian decided to climb up on a stool and get a Band-Aid.

Very soon, his parents returned home. They were, of course, appalled to learn what had happened. "Haven't you been told never to go into the medicine cabinet?" Brian's father asked angrily, his first response impulsive, impelled by his distress in the moment. As Brian cringed, his mother's first reaction was to blame herself. "I should have taken you both with me," she said. "It was wrong of me to leave you at home alone."

Brian's mind reeled in confusion and fear. He waited to see what would happen next, if he would be punished. But his parents quickly recovered from their shock and reassured him:

"We're very proud of you," his dad said in a calm and

soothing voice. "You did the right thing, taking care of your sister." "Yes, honey," his mom added, "you really handled the emergency well. But I still don't want you to go into the medicine cabinet—ever. I think we should move the Band-Aids to a place where you can reach them, in case you should need them again. But you're not to go near any of the medications in the bathroom."

From this kind of parental response, Brian was shown how to reason through a stressful situation. He learned that rules are sometimes contradictory, that there are occasions when choices must be made and decisions aren't perfectly clear. Fortunately for him, his parents demonstrated how to set priorities.

RULE 1: Take care of people who are hurt.
RULE 2: Don't go into forbidden places.

Brian had his first lesson in how to integrate incompatible principles, and he got a nice boost to his self-esteem.

As children reach their middle-school and high-school years and are ready for more freedom, many thoughtful parents establish a hierarchy of values to address the dangers of sex and drugs. Teenagers are told to abstain from sex and to "just say no" to consuming any intoxicating substances, but they're also told that should they find themselves in a dangerous situation in which they are fearful of sexual aggression or with others who are drunk or high, they should call home for help. Under such circumstances, parents promise that no penalty will be imposed.

In the long run, safety trumps being drunk or high or sexually victimized. Giving a teenager a pass on an occasion of bad behavior is better than finding him or her in an emergency room, suffering a bad reaction to substance abuse, or in the morgue after a fatal accident. Protecting children's lives by preventing the injury or death of innocent victims is the paramount rule. Drug and alcohol consumption and sexual activity are ranked lower.

Most adolescents are mature enough to understand how one good overrides another and how some bad behaviors are worse than others. Through discussions with parents and teachers, identifying with one another, and trial and error, most teenagers develop principles they stand behind, even in the face of pressure. But if this hierachy of values isn't established in adolescence, it's never too late.

HARRY: MAINTAINING SELF-RESPECT

Integrity requires thinking. If we simply follow the rules that have been established by others, we don't actually own our principles. Most of us learned our values at home, at school, and/or at a religious institution, but if we choose to live by those standards out of blind obedience or a desire to conform and be accepted, we have not achieved integrity. Optimum integrity consists of choosing personal ethical beliefs after careful and full consideration and adhering to them completely and consistently over time.

People with a high level of integrity are able to think

through troubling emotional issues quickly and arrive at firm conclusions based on self-owned, established priorities. And after reaching a decision, they are not riddled with second thoughts, struggling with subsequent doubt and anxiety. They know they made the best choice, given the circumstances and given who they are, even if that choice resulted in unfortunate consequences.

Harry, a senior faculty physician at a large urban university hospital, had spent a lot of time and effort prioritizing his values. His position involved enormous accountability to his institution, peers, patients, students, and support staff. He was called on every day to wear many hats: chief, teacher, mentor, employer, and friend. He knew well that these roles would sometimes overlap, collide, conflict, and present him with difficult choices. He did his best to psychologically prepare himself for these dilemmas by establishing a hierarchy of his responsibilities and principles.

He faced just such a sticky situation when it became generally known that two popular young doctors under his supervision had fallen in love. They were both excellent physicians with promising futures. Harry had the utmost respect for both of them, and it was obvious that they were well suited: equally mature, mutually committed to each other, and clearly blissful together. As their friend, Harry could easily applaud their relationship and be very happy that they'd found each other, but their liaison was strictly forbidden by institutional policy, and it was Harry's job to enforce the code.

To complicate the situation even further, these two

young people were more than just colleagues on the hospital staff. The young man was a junior member of the faculty and a direct supervisor of the woman he loved, who was an intern. The policy prohibiting an intimate relationship between any supervisor/supervisee was absolutely necessary to protect against sexual harassment and abuses of power. Although it was perfectly clear that those offenses were not an issue in this situation, this couple, nonetheless, was violating the institutional ethics Harry was charged to uphold.

In his mind, he knew his priority. He was committed to enforcing the administrative policy for the good of the organization and for the welfare of all his current and future staff. His first effort to address the issue was to meet with the couple and suggest that one of them transfer to another facility to resolve the problem. They both refused, insisting that they were each in the most optimum position for their careers. Harry had anticipated this response and wasn't surprised, but he was regretful, because he had to insist that this was the only solution he would accept.

The two became very angry and resentful, and Harry accepted their hostility with sorrow but without remorse, shame, or guilt. He removed both of them from the ward and assigned them separately to other locations. Noting this transfer in each of their records, he did not enter anything prejudicial. He had no wish to devalue the motives of the couple or demean them for their choices and actions.

Harry knew these two young doctors might continue to feel wronged by him, and he knew he was likely to be vilified and disliked for his exercise of authority by others on the staff, friends of the couple who sympathized with them, but that didn't matter. What counted for Harry was that he felt good about his decision, which meshed with his internal values and priorities.

Most of us have intuitive values. Being fully aware of what they are and why we hold them as our principles can help us use them wisely. Harry remained happy and serene, even in a stressful situation that cost him the goodwill of some of his coworkers. His principles were firmly in place—and in order.

RULE 1: Be an ethical doctor, mentor, and leader of the team.

RULE 2: Act in accordance with the rules of the hospital.

RULE 3: Protect the goals of the organization, which are to provide care, education, and research. If these goals clash, patient care comes before education, and both come before research.

RULE 4: Preserve my own well-being, in health, self-esteem, and the respect of others.

RULE 5: Be loyal to my friends, peers, subordinates, and trainees by honoring their desire for professional growth and personal satisfaction.

Harry could not satisfy all five principles. The situation meant he could act on principles one to four but not five. The couple that breached the policy—as understandable as it might have been—were unhappy with the outcome, but Harry, who knew his priorities explicitly, still took pride in his integrity, and justifiably so.

ROBERT: THE RELATIVITY OF VALUES

Finding coherent individual principles just within the space of our own minds can be remarkably difficult. So it's not surprising that when such considerations come into play in a larger arena, under the purview of a group of people, consensus isn't likely to be achieved.

Robert, an emergency-room physician, found this out firsthand from his colleagues in his workplace. As a doctor in a trauma center, he worked shifts, completing his assigned hours and then enjoying total freedom until he was on duty again. Many medical personnel consider this the most advantageous type of schedule, and Robert appreciated it too. In the ER, however, it meant that patients needed to be treated and either released or reassigned to another department in the hospital as quickly as possible, which sometimes conflicted with Robert's personal priority and commitment to give as much of himself to his patients as they needed.

On one of his shifts, when a severely injured child was brought in, Robert confronted this dilemma head-on. He treated the little boy's wounds, and then, true to himself, he gave a substantial amount of time and emotional support to the distraught family members. Later, a fellow doctor praised Robert for the empathy he'd shown to the boy's parents and siblings: "You have a lot of integrity to reach out to treat the whole family like that," he said.

Another coworker had a completely different slant on the situation. She thought Robert was lacking in integrity because he spent too much time with the boy's family when the ER was overwhelmed with urgent cases, leaving the rest of the staff to work under greater strain because Robert wasn't seeing his fair share of the influx of patients.

A hospital administrator agreed with Robert's coworker. He supported the rule that emotional support was to be provided in the ER by the on-duty social worker (who was paid less per hour than the ER doctors). When Robert's shift ended, the administrator reprimanded him, admonishing Robert to adhere to the rules in the future.

Each of these points of view has merit: Any good doctor knows the importance of timely empathy; all ER doctors know that they will sometimes be avalanched by patients and have to share the burden; and all administrators know that if a staff member spends too much time in one area, another area will be shortchanged. The judgments are valid, and the values are rational; the conflict is unavoidable.

Robert had chosen a course based on his principles and priorities, and he'd experienced the fallout. Now he had to reconsider his decision. Had he been right or wrong? And what about next time? Would he obey the administrator's directive? Or would he try to stretch the limits so that he might still be able to give himself as fully as he's needed and serve his own code? There is no easy answer. That's why adages such as *Always do the next right thing* or *Always do what's right* are nice but inadequate. Figuring out what's right in some situations can be thorny. This is where maturity, good judgment, and strong personal integration count. To know the self well, to have clarity about priorities, and to be psychologically prepared for conflicts that may arise is the road to solid self-esteem, self-assurance, and peace of mind.

Each of us must determine the order of our own priorities, and then we must resolve the question of how much we wish to commit to the collective values in our communities. For most of us knowledge of our morals and ethics is implicit. For instance, we intuitively honor the privacy of others in crowded places, such as an elevator, by not staring. Without thinking about it, we make many other good decisions about our public behavior, but thinking about it is exactly what I'm encouraging. For the journey toward greater psychological harmony and happiness, it's constructive to consciously reflect on these behaviors, and to know why we intuitively do the right thing socially, and to make implicit knowledge explicit.

The knowledge that refraining from staring in an elevator, keeping all eyes to the door, is a custom learned in childhood, taught by the example of parents and other adults is explicit as is the knowledge that this social convention protects everyone's boundaries. Turning implicit knowledge into articulate thought is the first step toward mindful, reflective decision making. These reflections show us how to braid many strands of competing values into a plaited whole rather than treat them separately, dissociating them. In addition, the ability to verbalize values paves the way for better communication, negotiation, and fair compromises with others.

Exercise: Making Intuitive Values More Explicit

1. Identify as many of your values as you can. Be alert to signals, both positive and negative, that a value is active within you. Which behaviors do you admire? Which behaviors of others push your buttons? If you are judgmental about an action or a motive—someone else's or your own—there's a value behind it. If you feel a sense of disgust or wrongfulness or, at the other end of the emotional spectrum, a sense of saintliness, heroism, virtue, or pride, there is an underlying ethic that you hold dear. Try to put it into words.

2. Once you can articulate a value, ask yourself:

- How was it developed?
- Who says it's so?
- Who shares it?
- Who might hold a contradictory value?
- Do you endorse it completely, or are you of two minds about it?
- Do you also hold a value that contradicts it?

- Are you comfortable with holding it and willing to be open about it?
- Would you rather not tell others that it counts with you?

These explorations will help you clarify the competing values in your mind.

3. Try to prioritize your principles. Consider several possible future scenarios that might present a conflict of values for you. Choose your priorities in each case. Consider how you would explain your hypothetical choice to someone who was critical of it. Rehearse your response.

A WORD ABOUT LOVE

When my patients and I work together on identifying and articulating their principles, "love" is highly likely to be near the top of everyone's list. We all attach great importance to love and invest ourselves heavily in giving it, getting it, and encouraging it in all areas of our lives. But what do we mean exactly when we say love is our value?

Contemplating this question was especially significant to my patient Edward, who consulted me because of the unhappy, frequently repeated cycle in his romantic life.

Edward was a young, rich, handsome, and very successful lawyer. He had no difficulty dating women, but he couldn't maintain a long-term relationship. His pattern was to pursue a woman, begin a relationship, and then reject her.

Edward was lonely and depressed most of time, except for those brief periods when "the chase" excited him. He was quick to enter into sexual relationships but unable to get closely attached. He'd never learned how. Yet he valued love, he told me forcefully, assuring me that he wanted to find it. So I suggested that we take a hard look at this value, rank it in priority, consider how it meshed with his sense of purpose, and measure it against his behaviors.

It took Edward almost no time to see that there was a difference between "love" and "joyous promiscuity." He recognized how he'd used rationalizations (aided by inebriation) to "cut himself some slack with women," as he put it. But by articulating his primary principles, by explicitly knowing what mattered most, he was soon able to change the way he navigated the world. Very quickly, he was able to exercise restraint in situations of temptation and consider the quality of his relationships with new criteria.

By the time we ended our work together, he still wasn't quite ready for the commitment of marriage, but he was able to stay in dating relationships for extended periods of time. Simply by verbalizing his values, he gained perspective and insight—and a new maturity that made him even more attractive to women at the same time it made him less likely to trade on his charisma. I had confidence that he'd continue to grow as a "man of substance" and that eventually he'd find his way to a stable, fulfilling, long-term relationship with the right woman.

BUILT-IN GUILT, BELOW THE RADAR

Some people have a very difficult job setting their hearts straight because, throughout their lives, they've been carrying what psychoanalysts call "unconscious guilt," a result of childhood experiences and long bouts of strain, stress, and distress. For a time, for these children, the world was a bad place. As mentioned before, when a child finds him- or herself in a painful situation, someone has to be blamed for it. Therefore, because of the natural self-centeredness of children, some of the blame gets lodged in the recesses of the mind, along with a foggy sense that these wrongs must be punished and paid for in some way in the future.

This burden can be carried for many years without ever becoming conscious. If put into words, it might sound like this: *Mommy and Daddy were bad to me, because I am bad. It's my fault the world is a bad place. I should punish me sometime in the future. I can feel good only after I've paid for all my past badness.* This latent sense of guilt and subconscious expectation of retribution interfere with the process of choosing good values. If an individual, within his or her own mind, cannot give the self the authority to be the central agent for determining what values to hold dear, it's extremely hard to reprioritize personal values in the way that is encouraged in this chapter.

If some aspects of this chronic but obscure guilt cloud your personality, you will get a hunch about this situation as you take on the lesson in this chapter. Emotions such as guilt, feelings of shame, or ideas that you must be a bearer of suffering will prejudice your view of integrity to the extent that your own values will be biased against you. Similarly, if you have projected blame for that badness onto others to cleanse yourself of fault, then you will find it hard to be reasonable in sorting out your values.

Your hunch will enable you to rethink your perspective as you work through the lesson. On fourth or fifth reflection, you may correct the notion that you always have to be blamed or always be the bearer of suffering. Making your unconscious attitudes clear to yourself can only help you on the road to happiness despite exposing you to painful memories or fantasies from your childhood. Professional help might be indicated, unless you can address them on your own, item by item. Dealing with particulars rather than generalizations is the topic of the next discussion.

❋ Teaching Points ❋

- Most of us have a committee of critics in our head, voices that represent different sets of values. It's well worth the effort to identify each competing lobbyist and to make your most rational self the chairperson of this contentious committee.
- Calm appraisals and mindful reflection can lead to creating an order of values that will be ready to serve you when you face moral dilemmas.

- Prioritizing values usually requires repeated effort. Putting your principles into words in your mind, writing them out on paper, or speaking frankly with a trusted confidant can often be helpful in achieving clarity.

Learning from Lapses

We all make errors and can learn valuable new attitudes from examining them.

Most of us have a moral compass. Sometimes, however, we head off in immoral directions. Self-gratification can lure us away from doing what's right. On occasion, we want what we want when we want it, whether we've earned it or not. A strong self-interest can eclipse our principles. Then, after committing an unethical or hurtful act, we feel guilt and/or shame.

Although it can be uncomfortable and embarrassing to think about our lapses, the process of examining our slipups can be a valuable learning experience. By making an honest appraisal, performing acts of remorse, and planning how to avoid making the same mistake again, we can offset embarrassment and earn a genuine sense of pride and self-respect.

I learned one of my first lessons about dealing with my mistakes at around age six, when a neighborhood friend of mine received a birthday gift—a cowboy set that included a gun with a belt and holster, a rope, and a sheriff's tin star—that filled me with envy. A couple of weeks after the party, while crossing the lawn in front of the boy's house, I came across that shiny badge. My friend had lost it in the long grass. I picked it up, hesitated for a moment, looked around, saw I was unobserved, then slipped it into my pocket and returned home, telling myself: *Finders keepers, losers weepers.*

Behind the closed door of my bathroom, I pinned the star to my shirt and looked in the mirror to see how it enhanced me. To my surprise, I did not feel glorious in my sheriff fantasy. Since I'd really pinched that star, how could I be the heroic lawman righting wrongs? Where could I show off? I might have wanted to accept that losing the badge was tough luck for my friend and fair gain for me, but, in fact, I didn't feel good about my new possession. It wasn't really mine; so I returned it. I went to the boy's home, knocked on the door, and confessed the whole story to his mother, a kind woman whom I respected. Then I handed over the badge. My friend, overhearing the exchange, rushed up, grabbed the star, and pushed me angrily. I just hung my head in further self-reproach.

His mother put a hand on each of our chests and said I'd done the right thing. She told me that I was brave and that it was good that I hadn't pushed back and gotten into a fight with her son. The praise filled me with pride. In a sense, I regained the happiness I'd lost in pursuit of what I'd envied.

What my friend's mother had done for me, we can all

do for ourselves when we consider a lapse. Whenever we use our reasoning to set ourselves on a firm course of principled action, we are on the path to peace of heart. It's the seventh essential lesson on the course to real happiness.

KEY MEMORIES

We are born with a need for social bonding, and we are hardwired to experience empathy and compassion. Then our moral compass is fine-tuned by our experiences in relationships and by lessons from parents, teachers, and mentors. Despite all this preprogramming for goodness, however, periodic lapses are inevitable.

Occasionally we all make mistakes, act meanly, betray a significant other, take what doesn't belong to us, etc. If we responded with perfect reason, we would immediately own up to our errors, figure out why we'd behaved badly, eject the thinking that led us astray, and move forward as new and improved people. But we often don't respond with perfect reason. Instead, we deal with guilt and remorse by not dealing with it. We might pretend we didn't make a mistake: *I did not intend for that to happen. It's not my fault*, we might think. Or we might shrug it off by saying "to err is human." Or we might blame someone else for our lapse, or protect the self from facing responsibility with rationalizations.

Our ability to rationalize our choices and actions through self-justification can be boundless, and as long as we continually deny our role in our problems of the past, we can't solve our problems of the future. As long as we are stuck rationalizing our past choices, those rationalizations are going to influence our present.

In his aptly titled novel *Therapy*, David Lodge has created a middle-aged character who comes to a long overdue recognition of how this dynamic has affected his life. This fellow's first teenage romance ended because the girl had had religious scruples that stood in the way of the young man's wish for a sexual courtship. Frustrated at her refusal to give in to his desires, he broke off their relationship. Years later, in his memoirs, he writes: *In the past, whenever I thought of her—and it wasn't very often—it was with a fond, wry inner smile: nice kid, first girlfriend, how naïve we both were, water under the bridge, that sort of thing. Going back over the history in detail, I realized for the first time what an appalling thing I'd done all those years ago. I broke a young girl's heart, callously, selfishly, wantonly.*

In reviewing old memories and grappling with the lingering sense of remorse, the character arrives at a new understanding. He writes: *You could say that it determined the shape of the rest of my life. You could say it was the source of my middle-aged angst. I made a choice without knowing it was a choice. Or rather (which is worse) I pretended that it was her choice, not mine, that we split up. It seems to me now that I never recovered from the effect of that bad faith. It explains why I can never make a decision without immediately regretting it.*

For Lodge's character, selfishness leads to years of regret. For many of us, self-blame, like guilt, can linger. We can consciously or subconsciously punish ourselves for something in the past, and thereby deny ourselves happiness because deep down we feel we do not deserve it.

Whether we pretend we're blameless, harbor self-blame, accuse others, or try to rationalize away our mistakes, we are failing to learn the valuable lessons available to us in our lapses. And failing to acknowledge mistakes makes for narrow-minded, self-righteousness that ultimately hinders our ability to be happy and find an enduring inner harmony.

HOPPER: REGAINING HAPPINESS

Hopper sought my help in his mid-twenties. He was working near the bottom rung of a corporate ladder that he hoped to quickly ascend, and he was doing quite well. Work was not a problem; however, for two years he had been feeling restless and sour without being able to identify any clear reason.

We began our work together by exploring his self-concepts and his patterns in relationships. Within a short time, he revealed that he'd had a recent liaison with his best friend's girl. His buddy had been out of town when Hopper had dropped by his house and was invited in by his friend's girlfriend for a drink that had led to unexpected and "pretty hot" intimacy. It had been by "mutual consent," Hopper was quick to tell me.

"Maybe it was okay," he went on; "I was horny and she was horny, and she and my friend are not married." But he was uneasy now about how his friend might feel about this episode, and as he spoke I could hear a note of chagrin in his voice. "Okay, okay," he said, "betraying a friend's trust is bad, and this could ruin our friendship, if it came out. And our circle of acquaintances would probably side against me, too, if what happened became common knowledge or even rumored."

At this point, Hopper's values regarding this episode now became the important topic of our work, but when I pressed him, Hopper became reluctant to delve deeper. We were wasting time on a small matter, he said. He was feeling almost insulted by my challenge to him to stay on this topic.

I said he was being evasive because he had a conflict, but in his own mind, not with me. I had said nothing critical, yet he was feeling criticized. "So let's look at this from all the angles," I suggested. "How do you feel about yourself in this situation, about your friend, and about the woman? Let's pull all these threads together and see what we have. What are the short-term pluses and minuses for you? What are the long-term consequences?"

Since Hopper worked in accounting, he was comfortable thinking in terms of numbers and percents. He said that adding another woman to his list of sexual partners was a positive memory and a twenty-five-percent advantage, but the uneasiness he felt about the memory ranked at around seventy-five percent. As for his male friend, Hopper had ten-percent pride at stealing the fellow's girl (winning a sportlike competition) and ninety-percent pain at having betrayed him. He was going to feel awkward around the woman forever now, so that was a one-hundred-percent minus.

"Well, those percentages make it pretty clear that your short-term gain in this episode is at the expense of a big long-term loss," I pointed out.

Hopper agreed. "I guess I lapsed in my own principles," he said.

Just using the word *lapse* helped Hopper. The label clarified for him both the episode and his own attitude. He now felt more in charge of himself. With his new self-awareness, he would be better equipped to handle similar situations in the future and to act more consistently with his own best interests and in harmony with his values.

GETTING PAST FIRST RATIONALIZATIONS

It's not always easy to do the right thing, but it does bring greater peace of mind and greater self-pride when we act with integrity and remain true to our principles. Matt demonstrated this truth when he found himself in a dilemma one night. Pulling into a narrow parking space, he bent the fender of his car and left a deep scratch on a stranger's vehicle. It was a big crisis because Matt was a graduate student who was living on a very tight budget and had no auto insurance. He was pretty sure that the damage to the other car would run into hundreds of dollars that he couldn't afford.

So he wrestled with what to do. He'd once had his car dented in a parking lot, and whoever had been responsible for the damage had simply driven away. People drove away from such accidents all the time. He could leave the scene now, and no one would be the wiser, except that he'd know, and Matt prided himself on obeying laws and being a responsible and contributing member of the community. He just wasn't happy with the rationalization that "everybody does it." Matt, sadly and reluctantly, left a note on the windshield of the other car, explaining what had happened and providing his name and number.

Sure enough, it was an expensive decision. The other driver got in touch, got an estimate for repairing the damage, and informed Matt that the repairs would cost four hundred dollars.

Matt borrowed money on his credit card to pay the bill. It took him months to pay it off, but as he scrimped and grumbled to himself about the hardship of the debt, he also felt the peace of mind he gained from keeping his internal record clean. Abiding by his principles made him happier than having more cash. He could like himself, sleep well at night, and know that he was a man who did the right thing, even when no one was looking.

For anyone arriving at a clear choice such as Matt's, the benefits more than outweigh any temporary cost. Whenever we act on principle, we strengthen our integrity by reinforcing the values of our conscience and thereby making future decisions in similar situations easier.

HELEN: A SUDDEN AND SUBTLE LAPSE OF JUDGMENT

Sometimes mistakes are blatant: It's clear even before we act that we are taking a misstep. But sometimes our errors sneak up on us. We act spontaneously, in the moment, and we may not even be sure immediately that we are in the wrong. It can take time and careful self-analysis to understand how we lapsed and then to decide how to rectify the situation and restore harmony, personally and with others. Such was the case for Helen, when she was caught off guard, spoke abruptly, and only later heard the whispers of her own conscience.

An executive in a farm machinery manufacturing company, Helen held an important corporate position. Over the years, her supervisors had rewarded her performance with praise, promotions, and raises, and she was well respected by the staff. She had the maturity and experience to be an effective manager, and she took pride in her professional behavior toward subordinates. She was careful to give every member of her team an equal voice, and she tried to exert her authority only when it was necessary. When she made a leadership decision, she always explained her reasoning, acknowledged the opinions of others, and gave credit generously where it was deserved. But one day, in a brainstorming session, she slipped in her professional manner and acted out of character, surprising herself and damaging her relationship with her colleagues.

Her team was focusing on determining how much risk the company would be undertaking by increasing the production of tractors. Because everyone trusted Helen, they expressed their opinions candidly and vigorously. Sam, a midlevel manager, spoke about the dangers of expanding production too quickly. He said that the projections Helen presented looked good but that they were based on unverifiable and overly optimistic projections of increased sales. From his analysis, which he presented with charts, he predicted that increased output would overextend the company and result in losses.

Helen was annoyed with Sam and his charts. She felt an impulse to call him a wimp, because he waffled so often and encouraged caution. She restrained herself from speaking her full mind, but she conveyed her irritation nonetheless by dismissing Sam's charts with a wave of her hand and speaking in a loud, sarcastic voice. "Our success depends on bold moves rather than on endless and excessive calculations," she said. Then she stood abruptly and walked out of the conference room, ending the meeting.

Back in her office, she thought about what had happened. She realized she'd humiliated Sam and she regretted speaking so harshly, but she did believe he was overly cautious and pessimistic. Yet, he was only presenting his ideas in a manner she herself had encouraged and doing his job with his mathematical projection of risk. *I won't say such things again*, she promised herself. Then she turned to other issues.

Later in the day, she met Sam in the hall and apologized for speaking so abruptly, trying to repair their work relationship. In the next meeting, she was especially attentive to alternative ideas, trying to reestablish group coherence. A short while later, she gave Sam a positive performance review and recommended him for advancement. Sam acknowledged her support and expressed his gratitude.

Helen felt the incident was totally behind her. The group was working well together again, her professional relationship with Sam had been repaired, and what Helen regarded as her lapse of responsible leadership could be forgotten, except she didn't forget about it.

She felt better, safe and confident that she had regained the respect of her team, but she continued to be plagued by intrusive memories of the episode. She was still ashamed of how she'd insulted Sam, but she also felt angry at him and somewhat fearful of what others might still be thinking and saying about her rude and unusual behavior. She was concerned that she might repeat such an episode, despite her resolution that she would not. These thoughts revealed to her that she had strong feelings churning within and that there was an issue here that she needed to clarify and understand. She decided she could use help figuring out what was going on, and she brought the problem to me.

At first, while describing to me what had happened, she used rationalizations: "I wasn't myself that day," she said. Then she assigned part of the blame to Sam: "His timing was bad, and he can be so negative and fearful." But almost immediately she admitted that this wasn't true, and she recognized that she needed to scrutinize the memory more closely.

My role as Helen's therapist was to guide her in thinking through the "Sam incident" step by step, a process that most people can learn independently. Professional assistance isn't required, but an understanding of the method is. It begins, as do all of the exercises in this book, with establishing a calm and open frame of mind. This state has been described in various cultures as higher mindfulness, introspection, or reflective consciousness. In essence, it's a highly aware mind experiencing itself thinking, feeling, and appraising. The key is to analyze without rushing to judgment.

For Helen, the first step was to think through the cause-and-effect sequences that had led to her lapse. In other words, to tell as accurate a story as possible about what had happened, including what she had intended to accomplish by behaving the way she did and the effect her choice of behavior had had on others. To do this, she had to admit that she had been abrupt and rude, that Sam had not been at fault in any way, and that she had left her team feeling baffled, off balance, unexpectedly vulnerable, and wary. She'd shaken their trust in her, and she'd surprised herself, creating new self-doubt.

Next, I asked Helen to reflect on the circumstances in which this type of lapse might be repeated in the future. I guided her to examine a range of scenarios, including her dreaded fantasies of a catastrophic outcome, her desired fantasies of an ideal outcome, and then a more realistic view somewhere between the two. As I've discussed earlier, by identifying the extreme edges of the fears and dreams in our mind (which are highly unlikely to occur), a more realistic middle ground can be illuminated.

When Helen used this method of contemplating best, worst, and middle-ground scenarios, she first spent some time thinking about what she most desired. Eventually, she was able to articulate that her dearest wish was to lead in a way that established mutual respect and fluid teamwork. She wanted to teach and nurture the people she supervised. With some embarrassment, she was also able to uncover her desire—human, understandable, and rather unrealistic—for the adoration of her colleagues.

And what did Helen privately dread? She feared being too authoritarian and consequently hated or feared. Even more, she feared that others would see her as weak and ineffectual. Helen realized that when Sam had presented his expert mathematical projections, she had felt ashamed. Helen lacked confidence in her math skills. In high school, she'd thought of herself as "mathematically weak," and she didn't think she'd reached the level of math proficiency in business school that she believed an executive required. She was fearful that her defect would be discovered and that as a result, she would be judged unqualified for her job, much less a candidate worthy of promotion to higher executive status.

Most of the time, Helen kept this sense of inferiority buried deep beneath the surface, but Sam had provoked it with his charts. For a microsecond, he was the enemy who threatened to defeat her, and she had shamed him as a defensive counterattack.

Having looked at her desired and dreaded scenarios, Helen acknowledged the paradox: By trying desperately to maintain the respect of others, she had caused her own embarrassment. She now considered the more realistic space between the poles of her wish for respect from others and her fear of feeling humiliated. Helen knew that, in spite of her fears, she was good at her job. Even her math skills were good enough. She was not perfect, but her record of achievements demonstrated her capability. She also saw that she was still vulnerable to triggers that could activate her sense of inferiority. She had covered her vulnerability by placing Sam, rather than herself, in the inferior position, but in the future she would find a better way to respond in similar situations.

Imagining how she'd do that, she installed an internal warning system, like a dashboard light, that would blink when she found herself in circumstances where she might face criticism. She hoped to recognize the potential dangers in the moment and then to brace herself to remain calm and self-aware, to check her tendency to exaggerate the threat and lash back defensively, as she had with Sam. She made a plan to delay any such impulses, giving herself time to generate a courteous response rather than blurt out either a defiant or self-debasing statement. She planned to protect both others and herself from further deflations in self-esteem in the future.

Helen rehearsed possible future scenarios. She imagined a meeting in which she was told that her facts were wrong, and she drafted possible scripts that contained appreciation for whoever made the point and her acceptance of responsibility for making the appropriate corrections. Helen practiced her lines in a calm, confident voice: "There is a problem. Let's gather all the facts during the rest of the day. Then we can reason out what to do together at our next meeting." She also practiced saying "I see the problem, but I need to analyze it further. Let me think about it and come back with some possible solutions." She visualized how she'd present herself, her posture and expression, and how she'd convey a self-confident seriousness, with respect for her colleagues and their ability to cope with a problem and achieve a good outcome, in spite of moments of sharp disagreement.

By recognizing and confronting the memory of her lapse, using calm contemplation rather than self-condemnation and revulsion, Helen grew personally and professionally. She used her lapse as a springboard to learning and gained greater confidence, self-esteem, and happiness.

Exercise: Thinking Through a Lapse

STEP 1: Review the memory of your slipup calmly. Examine the cause-and-effect sequences and your motives. What triggered you to behave badly? What effect did it have on others?

STEP 2: Identify the circumstances that led to your lapse.

STEP 3: Imagine similar situations that could occur in the future that could trigger you to act immorally or unethically again. Consider the possibilities that you most dread and then imagine your most desired outcome. Identify what would bring catastrophe and what would be an ideal outcome. Label these scenarios—best,

---

worst, middle versions—and label your role. Were you acting as your dreaded self, your ideal self, or as a realistic version of yourself?

STEP 4: Compare and contrast your rational and irrational attitudes. Make a realistic plan for your future behavior. Visualize yourself acting with self-confidence and self-control in a similar situation in the future. Rehearse and role-play a new script that reflects your adherence to your principles and values.

STEP 5: Apologize to whomever you may have hurt and offended, if possible. There is a skill to apologizing appropriately and effectively. First, keep your eye on your aim to restore a good connection. Suppress any temptations to continue to express anger or place responsibility on someone else. Instead, highlight the values you share. Maintain your self-respect and personal boundaries. You don't have to spill your guts in a huge confession, but you should explain your motives, if you can, and give realistic assurance that you will behave differently in the future. Describe or negotiate any acts you will undertake to restore amicability or to make reparation.

When you are apologizing to a child keep in mind that you are a role model teaching the value of owning up to mistakes and how to make amends.

❧ Teaching Points ❧

A systematic way of learning from lapses emphasizes conscious contemplation rather than efforts to shed blame and avoid the truth. Expanding your thinking allows you to arrive at new, creative solutions to old problems. Learn to tolerate shame and guilt and use these feelings for self-motivation rather than self-flagellation.

- Look for a balance between extremes of finding yourself totally blameless because others are at fault and excessive levels of self-condemnation. Project a similar context into the future. Think and plan what you would do differently.
- Rehearse your new plans. Include a stance of increased self-monitoring until your new ways become automatic.
- Remember the Five *R*s
  1. *Reconsider*: Call the memory back for review.
  2. *Reperceive*: Tell yourself the facts again; try to recall the correct sequence of events.
  3. *Reappraise*: What were the cause-and-effect aspects of this sequence?
  4. *Revise*: What did you do that you would now do differently?
  5. *Rehearse*: Practice your plan for the future.

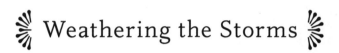

PART FOUR

Weathering the Storms

Breaking Through Roadblocks

*Illuminate obstacles that stop you from moving
ahead and find a way through them.*

Shame, guilt, fear, rage, and sadness—no one *wants* to experience these emotions; they're uncomfortable, painful, and at times even excruciating. Since it's human nature to avoid what is difficult and stressful, to gravitate toward an easy way out, most of us have learned by trial and error or by copying others how to block distressing states of mind. We all tend to develop defensive tactics that we habitually call on to deflect the intensity of unpleasant feelings.

These habits are seldom clear to us, perhaps they are even unconscious, but the more we can identify the patterns of behavior that we use to avoid our emotions the more likely we are to reflect on distressing thoughts and feelings from an objective perspective. Only can we uncover and illuminate the distortions and avoidances that impede personal growth, employ tools to counteract them, change ingrained habits, and become more liberated and more at peace.

Remember Adele in Lesson 2? She was scarred inside and out by a fight between her parents that ended with a flying pot of boiling spaghetti. In her six-year-old mind, she concluded that anger was so dangerous she had to put a lid on it for life. She became an adult who blocked any thoughts that might provoke anger, which made her an excessively meek and withdrawn woman... until she revised her "never-get-angry" plan. In therapy, she realized that "anger can be good or bad, depending on the circumstances and how it is expressed," a conclusion that freed her to reveal her feelings more openly and brought her more pride, confidence, and happiness.

We all store a collection of vivid images in our minds. Early experiences remain etched in memory, even if they may be deeply buried and seemingly long forgotten. As children, we may have formulated attitudes and operating tactics to avoid any repeat of some painful occurrence. In early childhood, irrational thoughts are developmentally appropriate. Ideally, in adolescence and later maturity, these give way to more rational thinking, but sometimes we get stuck on an idea and never get around to revising it. It's not unusual for an irrational attitude to remain in an adult mind, unconscious, dormant, yet readily activated by circumstances.

Most of us have an intuitive sense of when we are trying to avoid a distressing topic. Perhaps a memory keeps emerging, arising as an intrusive fragment of thought or appearing in dreams or in a visual image, demanding attention, expression, and review. Or we might also avoid disturbing subjects by indulging in aimless activity. I periodically find myself deflecting worrisome issues by raiding the refrigerator. I sift through food choices as if I'm starving and then toss every option aside, because, in fact, I'm hungering for "something else."

Attending to an unresolved topic requires deep thinking about it and then reflection on the thinking itself. As with every exercise in this book, the attitude with which you undertake the work is crucial. You need to be non-judgmental and calmly reflective. A sense of guilt and self-blame, feelings of helplessness and hopelessness, or a self-righteousness point of view isn't going to be helpful. These states of mind can tip you into too much emotion, short-circuit your efforts, reinforce your reasons for avoiding the topic, and may even bolster your continuing belief in unrealistic fantasies. To accomplish your goal, you need to take an objective view, unclouded by shadows from the past. Fortunately, it's never too late to become aware of an irrational attitude, eradicate it with mature reasoning, and then, forever after, enjoy life more without it.

CARL AND THE TOXIC TWINS:
SHAME AND BLAME

When he first came to see me, Carl, the twenty-five-year-old manager of a laundromat, was in pain, depressed, lonely, and drinking too much. His girlfriend, Lorna, had recently left him and quickly begun a new relationship with another man who was a member of their social circle. Carl was deeply angry at Lorna's sudden departure.

She'd left him without any warning or discussion, and since her departure she'd refused to take his calls. She didn't want to talk about what had happened. He was reeling from feelings of betrayal and totally mystified about how their relationship had collapsed.

Carl met Lorna at a bar where she waiting tables. After a few months of dating, they moved in together. There were tensions from the beginning. Carl and Lorna had seriously different wants and needs and conflicting ideas about their roles in their home. They disagreed on how to share responsibility for household chores and errands. Neither had skills for negotiating their disputes. After an argument, one or both of them might sulk for days. Eventually, they would make up, and then sexual intimacy would be restored.

When Carl began discussing this with me, he had difficulty verbalizing his attitudes. He did not see that he had any responsibility for the breakdown in his relationship. He blamed Lorna for every disruption in their domestic serenity. "I did my part," he told me. "I came home every night. I brought home my salary. I took care of the things around the place. I don't know what her problem was. She even refused to do my laundry."

"Did you expect her to do your laundry?" I asked.

"Well, sure. She was going to the basement laundry room with her own clothes. Naturally, she should be taking care of my clothes too."

"Do you think it's a woman's job to do laundry?" I asked him.

"Of course," he said. "I always assumed she'd do it, but

she thought that we should each do our own. She even suggested that I take my dirty clothes to the laundromat and wash them there."

They'd had a big fight over this issue. In fact, Carl had erupted with so much anger that it was clear the situation touched a sensitive chord within him. At first, he could not really think lucidly about why Lorna's resistance to doing his laundry was so painful for him. But in the supportive relationship of therapy, he was eventually able to acknowledge that her independent stance symbolized that he was not in control, not entirely "a man," much less the "man of the house." He felt diminished and shamed because Lorna did not do what he wanted. "I'm embarrassed at not being the man I thought I was," he told me sheepishly.

Shame was a feeling Carl habitually avoided and one he covered by blaming Lorna. Together, he and I looked the cause-and-effect sequences in the strains in his relationship with her. We examined his ideas about the roles of men and women, and we looked back on his experiences with earlier girlfriends.

I helped Carl expand his thinking and articulate his views. He began to recognize that he felt ashamed of his yearning for Lorna now that she'd left him. These sentiments seemed "unmanly" to him. He saw that his anger at her was a way to avoid feeling shame.

To help Carl get in touch with realistic thinking, we used the three-scenario method of looking at his attitudes toward Lorna. We began with his idealized version of how things might work out between them. In Carl's fantasy, Lorna still loved him. Their breakup was temporary.

She was missing him, realizing she had been unreasonably stubborn in her ideas about taking care of his laundry, and was ready for him to reach out in reconciliation. He would bring her flowers, and their harmony would be restored. She'd move back into his home and they'd never disagree about something so trivial as household chores again.

This scenario was extremely unrealistic, of course, but Carl smiled when he recounted it. It was an illusion that reinstated his sense of personal honor. In this daydream, he was a "real man" again.

His worst-case interpretation of Lorna's departure ignited a firestorm of fury. In this train of thought, Carl viewed Lorna as an evil seductress who had used him as a stepping-stone to get to the man she was with now, who had a better job with a bigger paycheck than Carl did. She did not care that she'd hurt Carl. She was climbing the social ladder, and she had no scruples about achieving her goals.

While relating this fantasy, Carl felt a rush of rage that gave him a burst of energy, empowering him, making him feel strong. It was a "he-man" flight of fancy that helped him to avoid a loss of self-esteem. It was also totally unrealistic, preposterous enough that Carl saw the absurdity in it and, for the first time, recognized his own irrationality. His idealization of Lorna—that she still loved him—and his demonization of her as an evil exploiter were both "silly" in his view. He saw them as irrational beliefs, and he was able at last to come to a more realistic appraisal.

At this point, Carl began to look closely at his self-concepts and to confront his sexist attitudes. He'd learned them in childhood, of course. "My father taught me that a real man should punish women who need to be taught their place. Any man who doesn't is a shame to his sex," he told me.

"*Mmmm...*," I said, "and what if I don't argue with you about that?"

"Then you'd be letting me get away with something that isn't working for me," he said.

"Well, now, I can really agree with you there!" I replied.

Carl had a lot of old ideas to ponder. He was able to explore realistic appraisals of himself and of why Lorna had abruptly left him. He realized that he'd never apologized to any of his girlfriends because admitting to a personal flaw opened floodgates of overwhelming shame within him. Once he saw this pattern, he was able to counteract it. He developed new skills of tact. He learned to apologize, negotiate, and accept responsibility without triggering self-loathing. He began to speak honestly and responsibly about his errors without feeling degraded and worthless.

He also worked on redefining what it meant to be a "strong man" and a "good woman." He became less inclined toward irrational and exaggerated blaming of others in what he came to call "a cover-up operation." He began to monitor himself for shifts in mood, to note when he was entering a zone of self-deception and self-righteousness, to give up his supposed moral superiority.

Carl was a good man with integrity and intuitive

values, the articulation of which helped him to modify his attitudes and to become wiser and more mature. By the time our work together ended, Carl had made an enormous shift toward becoming the man he'd always wanted to be, with a genuine ability to maintain happy and close relationships with full and tender communication.

Exercise: Overcoming Obstacles with Cause-and-Effect Reasoning

STEP 1: Analyze a situation; don't avoid it. Look hard at what caused the undesirable outcome. Consider how your needs and the needs of others interacted. What pulled you to act as you did? What pushed the people with whom you were in conflict? Ask: What might you have done that you didn't? Was poor timing involved?

STEP 2: Look for enduring attitudes and inappropriate, automatically learned values that you may be using to misinterpret many situations. These may become self-fulfilling prophecies if you don't correct them. When you do identify them, adopt a plan to counteract them. You are likely to repeat a train of thought that contains erroneous attitudes, so prepare for it by having a rebuttal ready. When your thinking drifts into the same rut again, repeat the rebuttal to yourself until, with practice, your automatic attitudes change.

THE SELF-RIGHTEOUS ZONE

Many of us, like Carl, avoid looking at our behavior and how it contributes to conflicts in our lives, and we can be just as reluctant as he was to look at the distortions in our self-image. We are wedded to a view of ourselves that we believe to be true and right and feel no need to let go of. Carl, fueled by anger, saw himself as a "wronged" man. He had entered the "self-righteous zone."

Like most of the people I've known in my personal life and my practice, I've been there myself at one time or another. It's a human condition—understandable, forgivable, and quite undesirable. For anyone interested in personal growth and greater happiness, self-righteousness is a major stumbling block to furthering any of those most important Three *I*s: (self-) Integration, Integrity, and Intimacy.

It is possible, though, to grow out of such self-defeating attitudes. I've seen many patients successfully triumph over sanctimony, pomposity, priggishness, grandiosity, arrogance, snobbishness, and self-satisfied smugness, to name just a few of the many ways we kid ourselves into inflating and distorting our self-image. I've had to catch myself in this quagmire and make the journey out more than once.

The first time I remember finding myself in such a situation, I was nine and in for a long ride before I realized the error of my ways. Because I was a bit rebellious as a child, my nonobservant Jewish parents sent me to a strict Catholic grade school. They expected the priests and nuns to reform my behavior.

This was a time when the idea that the Jews killed Christ still prevailed among parochial-school kids, and some of my classmates taunted me with the accusation that my ancestors had killed the one true savior of mankind. Despite the bad reputation of Jews, I made many good friends, and I was invited to become a member of one of the boys' clubs. The members of the other rival club mocked my acceptance by telling my buddies that I contaminated the group. I was angry, but I didn't let this ignorant heckling get under my skin. I simply concluded that anyone who belonged to the other boys' club was damned to hell for a lack of American values. God, I knew, was on the side of my club. Billy Hoskins, the leader of the other club and the school bully, believed as firmly as I did in God's support, only he felt it was on his side.

Billy sat directly behind me in class—we were arranged alphabetically—and liked to poke me from behind. His message was that I should move my head so he could see my paper and copy it; Billy wasn't above cheating. One day during a test, I deliberately supplied Billy with the wrong answers and, as I intended, our teacher correctly sized up the situation. She pulled Billy up from his chair by his ear and denounced him for cheating. Billy was humiliated, and I felt glorious, even after he punched me out at the next recess.

Our shared destiny, that alphabetic linkage, joined Billy Hoskins and me again in a public middle school.

We were now twelve years old. I lined up every day next to him as we awaited the arrival of our gym teacher. During the wait, Billy would say, "Let's practice boxing," and then begin smacking me with his fists.

"Why are you picking on me?" I'd want to know.

And Billy replied, "Because the Jews killed Christ."

I nurtured revenge fantasies. He was a bully, and I, in my daydreams, became The Avenger, a superhero. In real life, I attacked his parked bicycle, deflating both his tires by pressing in the air valves. He guessed correctly that I had done it and retaliated by stomping on my bicycle tires, breaking the spokes. I vowed counterrevenge, and the battle raged!

World War II was fresh in my memory. I visualized Billy as a Nazi who ought to be killed. I carried a pocketknife and imagined what I would do if seriously attacked. I idealized my wrath. As The Avenger, I was pure and good, but even though I was only a preteen, I still felt the other polarity. In my mind linked a shadow of self-demonization: I recognized that I was also a bully. Modeling myself after Billy, I picked on Henry, a smaller boy. But then, after giving Henry a bloody nose, I was filled with remorse.

I realized I had identified with the prejudice against me. In my demonization of Billy as a strong and powerful Nazi, there was also an element of idealization. I had fantasies of being a hero, but in them I was also being destructive. My revenge was fueled by my righteousness.

We were thirteen when we returned to school the following fall. I'd had a huge growth spurt in the summer months, and for the first time I was bigger than Billy Hoskins. I could become the bully—Mardi, The Avenger— for real! Because *Horowitz* continued to come before *Hoskins,* we were lined up next each other again. While waiting for our physical education teacher, I smacked Billy a few times, saying "Want to box?" Now that I was both smarter and physically stronger; he was in my power!

I enjoyed my superiority, but now I was just another bully, a role I had long detested when I was the victim. I could see Billy didn't like being hurt; I felt his pain. It was just like the pain that I had experienced at his hands. With this new insight, I began to take pleasure less in slapping him around.

I thought this over. Then I talked with my father, who suggested that I would get nowhere fast by trying "to get even." What really mattered was that I was able to protect myself from Billy. I should be "a boy of honor" and not bully anyone. He added that I didn't have to become Billy's friend; I could just avoid him. My father also said that it was better not to let a bully a triumph by becoming a brute just like him. The idea of allowing Billy to triumph was a huge new concept for me.

I let go of being pugnacious and belligerent toward Billy because that was his modus operandi. Mardi, The Avenger retired. Billy and I declared a truce, standing in line together, mostly in silence, or conversing superficially.

My family life was more peaceful than the Hoskinses'. Billy's father was often mean and abusive. I knew because

I had ears, and the family lived nearby. Now I know enough to speculate that Billy had an inner reversal of roles. Vulnerable and helpless with his father, he needed to subdue those he could dominate, as his father dominated him.

Billy was vulnerable to shame because he was so often demeaned by his father. He was a below-average student; it was only his unbeatable, bullying nature that gave him self-esteem in school. He satisfied his deep need for superiority by using his physicality to demean and dominate others who were more vulnerable. He rationalized his sadism by regarding others as inferiors who did not know their place.

Billy and I remained linked by our last names in high school phys.-ed. classes. When we were fifteen, we were teamed up to play in a two-man basketball competition. Exhilarated by our victories, we gave up conflict in favor of cooperation, planning tactics together, and practicing calling out signals to each other. After our competitions, we'd go out for ice cream and review all the plays. We planned new strategies and memorized new signals. We both left the self-righteous zone, which was lonely and isolating. We had a better relationship, although not an entirely friendly one. I now viewed Billy more realistically as a boy like me, but he still had his prejudices, and I had mine. I would only go so far and not give him the trust I gave my close friends.

Early in my relationship with Billy, I projected the fears I had of Nazis and their campaign of genocide against the Jews onto him. I exaggerated Billy's flaws and my virtues, as he had done with me. To further enhance my self-image, I cast Billy in the role of an evil brute, while I disavowed my own sadistic tendencies. Even when I enjoyed smacking him, it was because I was pure Avenger, teaching a bad person a moral lesson.

Today, as a professional therapist, I know Billy adopted the roles his father played. He became a bully to counteract his sense of great vulnerability. We're all like him. Even without an experience of early abuse, we all possess a wish for power and have the potential to be aggressive, whether or not we act on it. Who has not felt the flare of anger toward those who frustrate us, or envy of those we perceive as better off? It is unwise to pretend that we have no brutal tendencies; it is much better to acknowledge our aggressive feelings and then seek to govern them.

Self-righteous anger can *enrapture* us with *excitement*, but it is a snare and a delusion. It leads us to rationalize our aggression and give ourselves permission to express it. Recognizing this problem helps us avoid the trap.

VAUGHN: THE HELPLESS, HOPELESS ZONE

Oh, it's all beyond me. It's too much. I can't handle it. Recognize those words? We've all heard them. Sometimes, we might have been the person speaking them.

There can be comfort in giving up, a sense of freedom in letting go of all personal responsibility. When we experience the self as helpless and a situation as hopeless, nothing more is expected. When there's no need to try to overcome the problem—when coping is no longer an option—energy is conserved, and anxiety is relieved. It can be soothing to wallow in certain defeat. But it is another delusion, a swamp in which we can stagnate, a lonely place where no one will be coming to the rescue. Being aware of this zone and recognizing when we enter are important skills for anyone who values personal happiness. It's dangerous territory for peace of mind. Just finding yourself there should motivate you to slog out and move on, seeking professional treatment if necessary, if you're held there by depression.

Vaughn was trapped in this prison of complacent self-pity. He handled all his anxiety in life by giving up. Since he was no longer in a struggle for better relationships or a more fulfilling existence, he couldn't fail. Only the relief derived from opting out wasn't real. That's why he found himself alone and under the care of a physician who prescribed antidepressants for him and strongly recommended psychotherapy.

Vaughn, a freelance computer programmer, worked from home and interacted with others primarily on the phone or through e-mail. In his early thirties, he had no living family and no friends. He was shy and had difficulty making any kind of choices. He tried to stay in touch with his former college roommates and to develop friendships with some of his work associates, but these folks seemed to have little time for him and made no effort to return his calls. They acted as though he was irritating. He felt he got no sympathy and little respect.

To help make ends meet, Vaughn sublet rooms in his house to a single mother, Jane, and her two children. For some weeks, the arrangement was good for everyone.

Vaughn and Jane shared meals together and had many discussions about his work.

Then, one night, Jane asked him to sit with the children while she went out with a friend. He agreed. He was happy to be at home with the kids, preparing dinner together. He had them help chop vegetables, not realizing one of the children was too young for this activity. She cut her finger badly. Vaughn bandaged it, but that wasn't good enough for Jane. When she came home and learned what had happened, she was shaken and distressed. The cut wasn't bleeding, but it was gaping. Understandably worried, Jane rushed her daughter to the hospital emergency room, where a doctor stitched the wound.

Afterward, Jane berated Vaughn for underestimating the seriousness of the injury and for his bad judgment in putting such a big knife into the hands of such a young child. The next day, she moved out with her children, leaving Vaughn very alone and without a tenant to help with his house payments. He felt terribly sorry for himself and bitter at "the world" for how it had treated him. For several days after Jane's departure, he was in a deeper state of hopelessness than ever. He tried to work, but he was too glum to even surf the Internet with his computer. He roused himself enough to seek a doctor's help.

He was grateful for the physician's advice, although he didn't agree with it. He didn't want to take the prescribed medication, but he did visit a psychiatrist. After two sessions, he was told that he probably wasn't clinically depressed, but he did seem very constricted in his personality. The therapist recommended that they begin psychotherapy and that antidepressants could be reconsidered later, if needed.

For Vaughn, therapy was a significant turning point. With the support of his therapist, he was able to stop dwelling on his solitude, friendlessness, and hopelessness. For the first time, instead of staying in the trap of self-pity, he engaged in the work of constructive self-criticism. He started thinking about how others saw him. He was able to review lost friendships and to consider his expectations of others. He began paying attention to his sour moods, to monitor himself for whining and complaining. He worked at having friendly, superficial conversations with people he met around town and with those who gave him work assignments. He became more comfortable relating to others and developing relationships. Anxiety was still an issue for him, but he found he could tolerate it. Moving forward was bringing him so many new rewards. He was learning that the discomfort of inner tension was temporary and manageable.

Vaughn also considered how much responsibility he should take for the episode with Jane and her children. He decided that his motives toward the children had been well intentioned but that he had overestimated the hand-eye coordination of the younger child. He went to the ER and found out the cost of the visit. He wrote Jane an apologetic letter, accepting responsibility and wishing her and the children well. He enclosed a check to reimburse her for the emergency room services. He sent the envelope to the only address he had—Jane's mother's home. Jane did get the letter and wrote back a grateful thank-you. Vaughn felt good about that.

In the end, Vaughn was able to forgive both himself and his former housemate for what had happened between them, with a big emphasis on *both*. By starting a train of thought that led toward a choice, a plan, and then an action, Vaughn was able to leave the helpless, hopeless zone and start living a life of more quality and happiness than he'd ever experienced before.

FRAGILITY, INDECISIVENESS, AND PROCRASTINATION

Vaughn's case illustrates three common obstacles to happiness:

- a fragile sense of self or low self-esteem,
- difficulty in reaching decisions, making choices, and developing plans, and
- a tendency to procrastinate in taking effective actions or strengthening necessary life skills.

Each of these weaknesses is a handicap in itself, but when they interact, as they often do, personal growth can be seriously inhibited to the point of stagnation.

Vaughn obviously suffered from this fragile sense of self. He subjected himself to harsh self-criticism, which encouraged his social withdrawal and held him back from developing inner resources or skills for navigating the world. What he discovered in therapy was that these roadblocks could be overcome with action.

For Vaughn, as for so many patients I've known, the biggest first lesson was release from the weight of self-judgment. A social gaffe, even a misstep that is deeply shameful, may be embarrassing, but it doesn't have to be crushing. We all know that everyone makes mistakes. Yet many of us have difficulty extending that knowledge to ourselves. It is only when we increased our level of tolerance for the tension of uncomfortable moments that we can move on to work out effective strategies for recovering from errors. This is an essential task on the road to maturation, a common stumbling block not to be underestimated, and part of the work of a lifetime.

As Vaughn's self-acceptance and tolerance of his anxiety increased, his fragility, chronic indecisiveness, and procrastination all abated. His social skills, which would never come easily to him, improved. He discovered a previously unknown optimism within himself, along with a growing ability to think rationally, choosing a course, rehearsing steps, and then taking action at the right time, the right place, and with the right person. He became what he called a "growing-up man."

GAINING PERSPECTIVE

At some time, with most of my patients, our work together reaches a place where I talk about *bootstrapping*. A bootstrap is a loop of leather attached to the back or side of a boot to help pull it on. The term is often used as an adjective to describe a process of relying solely on one's own efforts and resources or, in other words, helping yourself unaided. I encourage my patients to use the concept of bootstrapping with their emotional thoughts. It's quite possible, I assure them, to climb up mentally to a level from which they can look back down, examine their feelings, see the roadblocks to their psychological well-being with objectivity and calm reflection, and then clear past them. And once an obstacle has been overcome, the road ahead looks much less dangerous and threatening. Disturbing thoughts, buried memories, disquieting images, and worrying fragments of ideas that have been covered in years' worth of mental detritus can be clarified, put in perspective, and definitely resolved.

Remember your tools to help you gain in self-understanding. These include the Five *R*s: Reconsider, Reperceive, Reappraise, Revise, and Rehearse. Another item in your toolbox is the three-scenario approach: By looking at the most ideal, most dreaded, and realistic outcomes of a situation, you can clarify your thinking. I've included several cases throughout this book to illustrate this technique.

An additional technique to expand awareness is working with three time frames. Simply put, by directing your thinking quite deliberately to the past, present, or future, you can design a new approach to handling issues in the here and now and thereby create a more positive future.

All of us have moments we look back on with regret and remorse. Perhaps we spoke thoughtlessly, behaved carelessly, or hurt someone unnecessarily. It can be acutely uncomfortable to remember having been a complete jerk. Our impulse is to hide from the thoughts, purge the recollection, and stifle the shame, a pattern that can easily become a habit. But as we become more self-aware and goal oriented, we need to learn a new cycle. When a shameful thought arises, we can recall it, accept the emotions it evokes, and then plan future behavior based on new, healthier attitudes. When our thoughts wander, we can ask ourselves: *What do I want to think about next: past, present, or future?* It is a simple yet immensely valuable strategy that puts us squarely on the path toward becoming "a person of substance" who learns from mistakes and moves on. It's the best any of us can do, and it is an essential key to happiness.

STATES OF MIND

Difficult memories, or a very hard topic to think through, require repetition of work that strives toward some type of completion of the emotional processing and belief changes that are involved. With all advice on doing this in a calm state of mind, the theme may press toward thinking-through in other states of mind. If you think about the theme in a saddened or demoralized mood the processing may move in excessively pessimistic directions, and if you do so in a mood of intoxicated exhilaration then the processing may move in excessively optimistic directions. It is helpful to note just what state you are in when reflecting on these hard topics.

It is sometimes helpful to name your recurrent states of mind, as in this is my "blah and blue state," this is my "happy as a lark" state. This helps you keep track of the contradictory beliefs about a hard topic that may emerge in your several states of mind. It also helps you notice your sense of identity; core beliefs about self tend to organize states, and beliefs about self may vary from state to state.

Naming states helps you tell yourself when you are having a transition in state, or when you are perhaps just about to go toward a state you do not want to have, that you may dread. Confusion is one such dreaded state; there are others, of course. Just having names for your states can be a bit of help in struggling to prevent an unwanted transition in your state of mind. Even if you cannot prevent some trigger from evoking a negativistic or out-of-control state of mind, having a name helps you remember what happened and what you thought during the unwanted state, and how that contrasts with what you think in a more desirable state, one with greater self-governance.

MOMENTARY CONFUSED STATES
AS AN OBSTACLE

If you are having trouble thinking about an issue, if your mind is just a jumble of thoughts, it's usually a sign that there's an obstacle. See your confusion as a signpost, not an impasse. Take it as an indication that it's time to rest now and do some sorting out later in a calmer state. Most frequently, the topic-specific state confusion occurred because positive and negative views were circling within your mind. Look deeper, and you are likely to see a dilemma. Try to put it into words. Unlike oil and water, you are likely to find ways to blend contradictions so that the polarities are less extreme.

In my experience, uncovering and changing attitudes and behaviors is not a "once-and-for-all process." Repetition is required. With any skill, the more you practice, the better you become. Self-observation is no exception. Regard yourself gently, as a "work in progress." Your review is "the story of my life so far." Focus your attention on a realistically optimistic future.

This set of techniques means taking a step-by-step approach and maintaining an attitude of compassionate tolerance toward yourself. "There I go again," you might say when you repeat an erroneous attitude.

Take a periodic overview of "the big picture." Be alert to hidden agendas or a lurking irrational life plan such as: *I'll be a good person when an ideal father takes me under his wing and tells me what I am meant to do.* Or a self-defeating mantra such as: *Because I am defective, I will eventually fail, so I can justify reckless driving. I don't have to sweat my responsibilities because my unhappiness will soon be ended.*

These statements may seem ridiculous written out, but I have heard such plans expressed many times. Reflective awareness enables you to reduce magical thinking and to use conscious beliefs to modify unconsciously held beliefs. Stating your plans lucidly through a positive, healing process of deep thinking and imagining helps you gain maturity and wisdom. A little more humor about yourself may also be helpful.

❋ Teaching Points ❋

- The more we can uncover habits that help us avoid our emotions, the more we can grow and achieve inner peace.
- Calm, reflective thinking can change distortions.
- Do not stay in the especially sticky zones of self-righteousness or self-pity. Look out for danger signals such as indecisiveness or procrastination out of a misguided sense of personal fragility.
- An emotional theme may have different meanings in different mood states. By comparing such views you can progressively integrate ideas.
- With steady practice, we gradually improve. Be persistent and patient.

Surviving Hammer Blows

*In the midst of winter, I found there was, within
me, an invincible summer.*

—ALBERT CAMUS

P ersonal tragedies, such as abandonment and betrayal,
as well as deceitful, exploitive, and malevolent acts by
others can leave painful, bitter wounds. Disasters, injuries, disabilities, deaths, and other traumas can change
lives forever. We naturally respond to these events with
rage, grief, and sorrow. These distressing emotions narrow our attentions to threats. After catastrophic upheav-
als we need to focus on changes and also eventually to
broaden our attention to find what satisfactions are still
possible.

In the first part of our adult lives, physical strength is
the greatest. During later adulthood, we're endowed with
high levels of psychological stamina. For those with the
strength and wisdom of emotional maturity, this stamina
is enough to keep us going.

When we have learned to handle stress, cultivate

gentleness with ourselves, think through pain, slow down the mind, and seek support, we have the tools to regain full happiness after devastating changes. By mastering these psychological skills, we can not only survive but also thrive, whatever the winds of fate may bring.

ELLEN: BEREAVEMENT

When Ellen suddenly lost her young son, she became a shattered woman who believed there was no possibility of future happiness. But she eventually discovered this wasn't true. She was able to emerge from her trauma, transformed, of course, by the journey through grief, but actually stronger, more confident, and more able to trust herself than ever before. Her marriage was changed, but it endured and became even more solid for having withstood the devastating tragedy.

On the first day of a family ski trip, Ellen and her husband, Max, took their two children on separate runs. While Ellen and seven-year-old Amy were on the beginner's hill, Max and ten-year-old Morgan took the chairlift to the intermediate run. At the top of the mountain, Max impulsively decided that he and Morgan should come down the advanced slope. While descending at high speed, the boy lost control, hit a tree, and died from a head injury.

Ellen's grief was overwhelming. For months, she was consumed with intense yearning for her son. She could feel nothing else. She was persistently agitated, morose, and irritable. She had no appetite and couldn't sleep. She consulted doctors about her symptoms and was treated for depression, which helped in some ways, but more than a year after her son's death, her grief remained crippling.

Ellen's rage toward Max and her revenge fantasies made healing difficult for her. She blamed her husband for Morgan's death, for the reckless choice he had made at the top of the ski run. *He should pay for his crime*, she thought repeatedly. She begrudged Max any moment of satisfaction or pleasure. A smile on his face, a hum from his throat would ignite a flare of fury within her. Occasionally, impulsively, she allowed herself to target him by throwing away his mail or "forgetting" his phone messages. This sort of nasty behavior was quite unlike her. She regretted it. She felt guilty and ashamed, but she couldn't stop. She valued her son more than her own life and, telling herself the truth, more than she valued Max. She loved Amy and wanted to shield her daughter from the ongoing tension with Max, but Ellen could not control herself.

Running through Ellen's mind were two conflicting themes. On the one hand, she thought: *Nothing will make up for the damage Max has done. It's right that he be punished because he deserves it.* On the other, she came up with the complete opposite: *What is done cannot be undone. Max is my husband, and I should suppress my rage for the greater good of my marriage.*

By the time Ellen came to see me, she had worked through many of the stages of her grief over Morgan's death. She wasn't clinically depressed, but she was still feeling remote from life and continuing to harbor persistent and intrusive revenge fantasies. We began Ellen's therapy by exploring her values and examining all her uncomfortable thoughts and feelings. She also, quite bravely and admirably, set a goal: to return to intimacy and happiness in her marriage. She was determined to make living well with Max a greater priority for herself than punishing him.

This was an arduous and ambitious task that required harmonizing many different elements in her mind. Ellen admitted aloud that she hated the impulsive self-centeredness of the man she married, but she loved his many good traits: his quick mind, sense of humor, compassion, generosity, and love of family. She could acknowledge that she and Max both mourned their son, and she was able to feel compassion for the remorse and terrible burden of responsibility her husband suffered because of his poor choice. She admitted that Max was both strong and weak, good and bad—a key recognition that finally allowed her to integrate and harmonize her feelings for him.

Eventually, Ellen was able to give up on revenge; she called her new stance of "grace and forgiveness." She took pride in her achievement of this enormously difficult goal, which increased her self-esteem—an important component of successful living after enduring catastrophic stress—and enabled her to trust herself more. Although she still felt somewhat numb and insulated, she became less depressed and apathetic and, as a result, was able to experience more varied states of mind, including hope, joy, and love. Returning to feeling fully alive, however, took more time. She continued to struggle with a sense of unreality, of detachment from the world and from her self—signs that there was more work to do. She had many conflicting thoughts and emotions remaining to be explored.

Ellen was willing to examine and reexamine her loss and what it meant to the rest of her world. She looked at her fantasies and realities, acknowledged both, and explored their differences. She revised her expectations, intentions, goals, and plans; reviewed her philosophy of life and death; and reevaluated and sorted out her spiritual beliefs, morals, and values. She also reconsidered her relationship with God and her religious community.

Ellen took a thorough and complete inventory, and, in the course of it, she was gradually more and more able to accept my support and empathy in therapy. In time, she was able to accept support and empathy from others. And she began to receive much more support because she became less remote and hostile toward her friends and family.

Max also changed: He matured, thanks to the insights he gained from his long and personal journey of suffering, remorse, and mourning. But it was Ellen's emotional shift, her success in reaching across a painfully wide chasm to embrace both the love and the hate she felt for her husband, that restored the affection, intimacy, and stability in their marriage. Together, Ellen and Max were able to move on, to find new meaning in their lives, and to claim inner peacefulness again.

Exercise 1: Navigating Life's Greatest Emotional Challenges

Extreme stress disrupts equilibrium. Sometimes tragedies happen suddenly, clobbering us over the head. Sometimes catastrophic changes can sneak up quietly, overtaking us subtly. Sometimes we may be in a profound state of grief without even knowing how we got there.

Finding a way out of any state of unbalance requires that we first identify the cause of the problem and then gather the physical and emotional resources to manage it. Like any other journey in life, to move through and beyond trauma, you will need directions, supplies, plans, and, most of all, support from others.

STEP 1: Be Alert to the Signs

Extreme stress from any cause can result in one or more of the following:

- repeated intrusive ideas and feelings that do not seem to progress toward resolution
- an uncharacteristic remoteness from others
- an emotional flatness or numbness
- a sense of the unreality
- a sense of the self and/or the world as gray, unimportant, or insubstantial
- a degraded sense of self

- flare-ups of irritability
- a sense of childlike helplessness
- imaginings of catastrophic scenarios when things don't happen as planned

STEP 2: Identify the Stressor

This may seem patently obvious if you've suddenly lost a loved one, or are the victim of a crippling accident or a natural disaster, or are experiencing the slow, agonizing decline of your own health or the health of a beloved one. But you might also be having sudden, sharp pangs of intense distress for which you only sense the triggers, in which case you must consider and sort through the mix of emotions on the inside. If a particular memory or event has resulted in intrusive thoughts or unbidden images, your instincts may tell you that you need to look at what's happening in your mind first. Maintaining a journal of thoughts, dreams, images, or even disjointed fragments of ideas can help bring order to what may initially seem like internal chaos. Be patient and gentle with yourself. Strive for a calm detachment. Try to observe your mental work objectively, without self-criticism, expectations, or consideration of others' opinions.

STEP 3: Identify What the Stressor Means to You

Remember that every traumatic event disrupts a person's fundamental sense of being. Do you feel "altered" in who you are? If so, how? Many concepts may be activated, some realistic and others fantastic.

Work hard to differentiate which is which. Examine and explore all the ways in which this event has forever changed your life, your thinking, your expectations, and your relationship to the world, to others, and perhaps to your creator.

STEP 4: Seek Support

Do not be afraid to get help. Sometimes working alone is just too hard. Support from friends, relatives, and/or a professional counselor can help you carry the burden and gain perspective. Others may help you clarify your thinking and differentiate between the realistic and the far-fetched.

STEP 5: Take Time Out

The work of recovery from trauma is long and hard. Along the way, you need to maintain and fortify your energy with sleep, recreation, and other self-care activities. Keep in mind that respite is not procrastination; you will be devoting more effort after a time-out has refreshed you. The journey is not to be made in a day, a week, a month, or even a year. Allow yourself plenty of time; there is no hurry to "get over it." Ignore any voices that urge you to rush. Recognize that others sometimes say or do things based on their lack of knowledge about overcoming trauma.

PETER: AGING AND DISABILITY

As we mature, our sense of identity usually becomes increasingly more solid, but a sudden insult or injury to the spirit can cause a regression, in some instances, all the way back to a childlike state.

"After the car accident, when my husband was pronounced dead in the hospital emergency room, I was in a state of shock and numbness," my friend Charlene recalls about suddenly being widowed at age forty-four. "I experienced a sense of total detachment and unreality that lasted a long time, yet there was a yearning from deep within me that I struggled to name. I finally identified it as a longing for 'Mommy.' It was startling to realize that I'd been vaulted back to the vulnerability of a toddler who could only cry out for the comforting arms of a parent."

Charlene's experience isn't unique. In an emotional crisis, our adult armor is often temporarily stripped away. But once the work of achieving mastery over the stress is underway, we usually revert back to our mature sense of self. During these regressions, some individuals can feel that they've become unhinged. Thoughts such as *I'm losing it. I'm going crazy.* can run through the mind. In some cases, a persistent sense of guilt, perhaps unconscious, can lead to thinking *I deserve this and worse.* In these circumstances, it's helpful just to recognize regression, to know it's an expected, natural, and transitory state in the throes of trauma.

There is, however, a danger of getting stuck in an earlier developmental state. Anger at fate, a sense of injustice, or just general irritation from pain and fatigue can start a vicious cycle of decreased maturity and increased dependency on others. This is what happened to Peter when his acute illness became a chronic disability.

At fifty, Peter began to experience symptoms that turned out to be the onset of a severe form of diabetes. His treatment required insulin injections as well as major changes in his diet. He was also told that he could expect to have complications in the future.

At first, Peter's stamina and courage in coping with his condition were good, and he felt supported by his friends and family, but then, over the next few years, his condition deteriorated. He developed vascular obstructions in his legs. At sixty, he was informed that at least one—perhaps both—of his legs would need to be amputated because of insufficient blood supply. He felt terrified, angry, and sad. He complained bitterly to his family and friends that his illness was unfair. They, in turn, felt miserable and helpless.

Peter recognized that he was alienating others, unfairly blaming them for his illness and frustration, and inappropriately directing his anger at anyone who was not infirm. He sought psychotherapy to help him cope with all the conflicting, overwhelming emotions over his plight.

In his heart what Peter really wanted was what everyone wants: to enjoy a long span of good health; to feel younger than his age; to be competent, vigorous, full of potential, invulnerable, and free of disability, magically restored to all the strength of his youth. He wanted death, when it came, to be swift and painless. He dreaded the opposite: to lose one bodily function after another and decline slowly, in anguish, totally helpless and dependent on others.

In discussing this dreaded scenario with his therapist, Peter gained an important insight. He realized that part of his despair over the future was his primal terror of being out of control, overwhelmed, and neglected. He was not envisioning himself as a mature, competent adult but rather as a helpless and uncared-for child.

Feelings of helplessness and abandonment weren't new to him. When he was seven and at boarding school, he'd contracted an infectious illness that resulted in his being transferred from the school infirmary to a hospital—a strange, frightening environment for a little boy who was left alone in isolation for long periods. Of course, the loneliness and desperation had been traumatic for him. These resurfacing memories, brought on by cascade of consequences of his disease, now frightened Peter.

Once he was able to sort out the past from the present and to articulate his most cherished (and quite impossible) hopes and his greatest fears, however, Peter could take stock of his situation realistically and deal with it calmly, maturely, and with as much wisdom as he possessed. He faced the truth about his future squarely, shying away from nothing. He knew that many of his days to come could be counted on *not* to be rosy. Although there were likely to be times of relative equilibrium and peaks of well-being, there were also sure to be low periods; troughs of pain, a steady, continuing decline in his condition, and likely assaults of fear and dread with each turn for the worse.

Considering how he would cope with his future vulnerability, Peter set as his goal to value each peak and to be as mentally prepared as he could for the onset of each valley. He could not expect to always be successful in this aim, but he set out to work on it, and that gave him hope. He knew he would have moments of despair as his condition worsened, but he also knew that medications for pain and anxiety management could ease his passage. He began to make plans for creating more time for self-soothing acts, such as listening to his favorite music, and for dealing with pain and disability before they happened, so that he could go on with his life the best way. He used the Internet to study diabetes and its treatments, taking an active role in his own care. And he became familiar with stress management techniques, muscle relaxation, and breathing exercises that he thought would be useful to him.

He let his imagination take him to the very end: He saw himself dying, not as a terrified little boy without inner resources but as a courageous man who could make his own decisions in each moment. He also considered the possibility of suicide as a solution if he were about to enter an intolerable terminal state, but since this was not his current situation and might never be, he made a commitment to refrain from any suicidal impulses during his low periods as long as there were moments of living that he still enjoyed.

All of this helped Peter to feel more in control and less preoccupied with the anxiety of imagined, impending disaster. He started to focus on the world beyond his own body. He now had a clearer grip on his destructive tendency to lash out when he felt pain, fear, or depression, and he was able to rein in his irritability as well as his demands on family and friends. The pride he took in his effort to live with a potentially terminal illness as gracefully as he was able helped to temper his resentment toward others who still enjoyed robust health. He began to think about his family's future and how he wanted to be remembered. He became determined to increase his positive relationships and to provide a role model for the younger people who witnessed his struggle. His new attitude relieved others of bearing his pain, and he benefited from their increased support and empathy for his suffering as well as from their respect for his courage.

By not giving up, Peter became the man he wanted to be: one who could cope with and endure suffering. He could see that others admired him for his fortitude, and he experienced great pleasure from moments of relief and escape and from the warmth of intimacy with others. The gift that he gave to himself with his rigorous honesty, integrity, and maturity was the ability to maintain his feelings of happiness and inner peacefulness, even during his most difficult times.

FACING THE INEVITABLE

It's been said that it is best to live long, remain healthy, and die fast. In other words, it's good to avoid illness and disability. But most of us have little choice in these matters. All any of us can really do to influence our fate is eat right, exercise, maintain good relationships, get good medical care, and avoid self-destructive behavior by not taking unnecessary risks.

If we live long enough, sooner or later, for a short or a long time, we are going to experience a physical decline. Even I am not so sexy in my bathing suit anymore. I have lost people I loved. My own risk of serious illness increases every year. Other senior citizens, perhaps retired, may have discovered to their dismay that their nest eggs and pension funds are not as substantial expected, or that their grown children, with their own heavy responsibilities, may not be as attentive as desired.

In one way or another, we all must eventually experience periods of steady, continuous decline—illness, loss, remorse, disappointment, and diminishing physical and mental capabilities—it's the nature of old age. I want to be clear in warning you that as we age, we can find it difficult to maintain relationships as well as our sense of purpose and meaning in life. But at the same time, I want to assure you, that we do not have to fear and tremble at the onset of these difficulties. Wisdom, humor, and realistic attitudes, along with the solid foundation of the three *I*s I have talked about throughout this book, are the only skills we need to master our circumstances. With them, our happiness is secure.

FRANK: STEERING THROUGH TRANSITION

Always an active and vigorous man, Frank was forced to retire at sixty-eight, after having worked for decades as a vascular surgeon. Now suffering from macular degeneration, which was constricting his vision, he could no longer perform surgery. He accepted his fate graciously, and planned to spend his time breeding dogs. He was, in fact, looking forward to slowing down and relaxing, to enjoying domestic life with his wife, and to visiting more with his children and grandchildren. But after the first few months of retirement, he discovered his lifestyle was not nearly as golden as he had anticipated.

Frank had always defined himself by his work, his hospital colleagues, his surgical skills, and his relationship with his patients. Now his sense of self felt shaky. His new hobby wasn't giving him the pleasure he'd expected, and without a set schedule and feeling of productive accomplishment each day, he felt restless, unhappy, and bored.

Worried that he might actually have fallen into a clinical depression, Frank consulted a former college roommate who was now a psychiatrist. This old friend didn't think Frank's problem was depression but rather his difficulty adjusting to retirement, which was a major disruption in of his equilibrium. First he suggested that Frank establish a set routine, so that he would not feel so adrift throughout his day. If Frank prepared a schedule the night before, he could awake each morning with an agenda already in place. Then he suggested that Frank start regarding retirement as a new life, instead of expecting it to be some kind of pleasant extended vacation.

This advice might seem quite simple, but it required a major adjustment in Frank's thinking, and it took real and sustained effort to implement. It meant that Frank had to construct new goals while facing up to his declining vision in the process. Even though he was not yet significantly impaired, now was the time for him to rehearse reading with a magnifying device so that he could still access information when he lost all central vision. He also had to plan how to remain mobile after relinquishing his license to drive. And he had to work on his new sense of identity and purpose and to talk more openly with his wife.

Frank, who was eager for a challenge, embraced this undertaking with gusto. He began keeping a journal of his experiences by dictating them into a tape recorder. Throughout his professional life, he'd recorded summaries of his surgeries and consultations. Now he talked about his everyday schedule, his activities, his thoughts, dreams, uncertainties, and insights. Every Monday morning, he'd review the tapes he recorded in the previous week and reevaluate the coming days based on his feelings and intuitions. He experimented with new routines, looking for ways to make his days more purposeful.

Frank decided to resume trips to the regional medical

center for lectures and discussions. He could not read the Power Point projections, but he came prepared to listen carefully and to join in when he had something to offer. He found this intellectually stimulating and meaningful, even though he was no longer engaged in active practice. Some colleagues called on him for advice, and he enjoyed their gratitude for his consultation. He deliberately spent more time listening to the problems of his children and grandchildren, supporting and advising them. Talking with his wife, Frank discovered that she was more interested in dogs than he had realized, so he shared his knowledge of the psychology and biology of canines with her. She reciprocated by teaching him about botany and gardening.

Like Ellen with her bereavement and Peter with his declining health, Frank worked hard to master a serious life event, first by recognizing the signs of being adrift, then by making a concentrated effort to shift his attitude and accept responsibility for his own experience, Frank found his way to new revelations about himself and those close to him, new pride in accomplishment, and an increased satisfaction and happiness with life.

Exercise 2: Thinking About Threats

No one wants to spend time with the feelings generated by abandonment, failure, and imminent threats, but when you take the time to think them through, you gain a clearer and more realistic perspective, which will help you devise the best strategy for managing them.

STEP 1: Select a Problem That Needs Sorting Out and Rethinking

What upcoming event or memory is disrupting your sense of balance or your sense of who you are? If you come up with more than one problem, examine each issue one at a time, from the least troubling to the most difficult and from the most quickly resolved to the one that you fear may take forever.

STEP 2: Clarify Your Dilemmas

Before you look for a solution, look for what got you stuck. Peter lost his way because he was overwhelmed by anxiety about a dreaded, unknown future, while Frank simply found himself adrift, bored, restless, and without direction. Consider where you want to find yourself: your ideal situation, your most dreaded scenario, and what is the most realistically possible outcome. Try to identify everything that is motivating you and how you expect others to respond to what you might do. Include your reactions to their possible responses.

STEP 3: Expand Your Associations to Each Horn of the Dilemma

Look at the connections. When Peter realized his fear was being fueled in part by a long-ago childhood trauma, he was able to master his circumstances. Expect unpleasant and unsettling feelings to arise as you explore your inner landscape. If you are ready to tackle the subject, you are undoubtedly able to tolerate the distress. Go forward with confidence, but if you do feel overwhelmed, hopeless, or out of control, take a time-out and seek some kind of calming restoration. You cannot rush; these problems are sticky and require patience. If necessary, consult a professional counselor as a guide.

STEP 4: Continue to Examine Contexts and Possible Scenarios

Tragedies, traumas, or the inevitable ravages of aging often mean making choices, in which case, the strategy of parallel and comparative scenarios is always a useful tool. Focus especially on differentiating what is likely and what is unlikely to happen as you examine the best-case, worst-case, and probable-case scenarios. For instance, if you're facing a dilemma as to whether or not to move to an assisted-living facility, consider all that you will gain by joining a new community, all that you will lose, and how the move will meet your needs and expectations in some ways but not in others. Make a divided list of pros and cons, of both going and not going. What are the needs, motives, and expectations of your family? What is causing your resistance? What would increase your flexibility? If it's time for a transition, how can you accept, facilitate, and even enjoy it?

Allowing yourself to learn the facts and to picture in your mind what the real consequences of certain decisions might be will help you separate reality from fantasy. Then you can answer these questions for yourself:

Are your expectations appropriate? Is it possible that you are repeating some error in judgment because it seems normal and so familiar? Are you imagining unrealistic, catastrophic outcomes?

STEP 5: Recheck Your Decision-making Process.

Your answers to the questions in Step 4 are likely to leave you with a clearer but still real dilemma after you assure yourself that you can tolerate more emotion than you previously believed, recheck for avoidances, impulsive choices, and distortions. Imagine yourself as your own wise teacher reviewing what you expressed. Try to correct dysfunctional beliefs. Now you can examine your priorities in light of the values you sorted out according to the exercise on pages 193 to 194. Make the right but not necessarily the easier choice and use it to plan your moves. Verbalize a phrase to use as a mantra, saying "This is the way I choose to go."

STEP 6: Consider Your Plan the Grounded Center of Yourself

If you feel that you have completed your work on the problem, memorize and repeat your positive phrase. When the problem intrusively pops up again (and it will), you can promptly refer to your mantra for a solution rather than worry. Remind yourself that you have thought the matter through already, realistically, and made your best available choice.

SHIFTING SANDS OF TIME AND SELF

Over a long life, the Three *Is*—Integration, Intimacy, and Integrity—change in their relevance. Early in adulthood, the emphasis is on getting yourself together. Then the emphasis shifts to relationships, which may include new intimacies with a child and with aging parents. As professional and personal development progresses in adulthood, greater power and authority both tests and strengthens integrity.

With advancing age, power is diminished. But even toward the end of life, there's a need to keep growing, revising values, and expanding spirituality. At this point, a sense of legacy will emerge, and thoughts about what you will be leaving behind will arise. Psychologically strong older adults who weather the storms of aging and adjust their attitudes to their situation and embrace their own mortality provide the younger generation with a meaningful model of emotional health.

When Peter decided to live as well as he could with his debilitating illness, he knew he wouldn't always be successful, but just making the decision to work on it gave him hope and, in the process, boosted his pride in himself and increased his happiness. His efforts didn't go unnoticed by those around him. Living life as fully as we're able is a very worthwhile goal and our best chance of reaping life's richest rewards, even if we sometimes fall short.

ME AND MY HEART

For many years, I had a heart murmur that did not need any treatment. Later, however, a routine, periodic echocardiogram showed that the valve causing the murmur had begun to give way and that my heart was in danger of soon becoming enlarged. My physician recommended a valve repair: open-heart surgery.

As a doctor, I know very well how risky a procedure this is. A certain percentage of patients don't survive it. Yet without the surgery, I was looking at certain death in the not-too-distant future. So, given my otherwise good health and the statistics of others with similar conditions, I chose to take the risks and agreed to the surgery.

When I told my friends, family, and colleagues about my impending trip to the OR, some said, "You are a world expert on stress. What is this like for you?" Well, I did know some truths about stress: No one is immune, and all of us will experience different feelings and thoughts when dealing with it. Sometimes we confront our feelings; sometimes we turn away, denying them for as long as we can. I knew that I would have some fears and that I should prepare myself accordingly. I also expected to experience periods of serenity, punctuated by bouts of tension. I reminded myself that my feelings about the surgery would fluctuate, depending on my mood, and this proved to be true.

My primary fear was not surviving the surgery. After that I worried about having complications that would

make it unsuccessful, or experiencing other complications such as loss of some brain function from clots,
anoxia, or anesthesia. My fears turned out to be partially
groundless because, according to the statistics, these risks
were actually not as great as I had imagined them to be.

First lesson: It helps to know the facts; we tend to
inflate the worst-case scenarios when we get bad news
and disregard our first sense of omnipotent disavowal.

As the surgery approached, my sleep was full of
dreams, which I used to examine my many feelings,
which kept popping up unbidden. In one recurring
dream, I was an artist observing the operating room
during someone else's heart-valve-repair surgery. My
focus was on how best to draw the scene. Since I wasn't
the patient, I categorized this dream as serene, and I was
grateful whenever I had it.

In another dream, I could not breathe. I'd wake up,
gasping for air, and I'd be reminded that when I woke up
from the actual surgery, there would be an endotracheal
tube forcing my breaths. I'd seen many patients hooked up
to that machine, dependent on that tube, and I knew it was
very uncomfortable. This dream was obviously all about
my fear, but as I reviewed the terror of it, I was able to turn
it into a comforting thought: that when I woke up feeling
that discomfort, it would mean that I was still alive.

In yet another dream, I was a child struggling with
the surgical personnel. I recognized that this was partially triggered by my memory of the surgery I had when
I was six. At that time, ether was used for anesthesia. A
slower means of putting a patient under, it sometimes

created a choking sensation that left many people with traumatic memories. I knew this dream was about my fear that something in the procedure would be too difficult to bear, forced on me by the people who were meant to be healing me. But, in thinking over this tense dream when I was calm and awake, I reminded myself that I was with a home team of professionals (at my own medical center) who were all on my side, and I relaxed into a level of somewhat uneasy serenity, if you can imagine that, a relative but incomplete security.

My concept of a home team was intended to my post-surgery care because of the prior arrangements I had made. Rather than putting blind trust in the hospital system (which, I know from experience, is quite fallible), and the staff (who can often be overworked and over-extended with responsibilities on the floor), I asked my family to stay near me in shifts during the first thirty-six hours after the surgery. I gave them a checklist of priorities to address and possible errors to guard against. These preparations left me feeling more in control, secure, and very appreciative and grateful to my loved ones.

A few days before the operation, my surgeon examined me. "If you don't hear a murmur, the whole deal is off," I told him, only half-joking.

After placing his stethoscope all over my chest, he looked me in the eye, put a hand on my shoulder, and said with some warmth, "I did hear the murmur."

The touch and the empathy were very reassuring. I had reached out, and he had reached back. That was important.

I also thought about what inner strengths I would need to call on to get through the tests, surgery, post-surgical pain, ups and downs in regaining my energy in the days after prolonged anesthesia, and so forth. I called these "courage and stamina," and this became my mantra. Whenever a wave of dread washed over me, I repeated this phrase to myself, and it worked beautifully, because I knew that the road leading to the end of this ordeal would not be traversed quickly. I should allow myself to work through all the tension, dread, and anxiety at my own pace. Repeating my mantra reminded me that I had made a reasoned choice and could therefore shrug off the otherwise endless ruminations of doubt in hindsight. I had already thought through my choices, and I was committed.

All of this preparatory thinking and having a mantra ready to counteract my repetitive tendencies to worry served me very well. It's much better than dealing (or not) with this kind of personal challenge by refusing to think about it beforehand, as many individuals do because it brings up so much anxiety. Careful preparation is a declaration of a strong self that, in and of itself, is gratifying and reassuring to know you possess, especially when approaching dire straits.

I recovered fully a few weeks after the surgery. When it was all over, seeing my chest scar in the mirror continued to surprise me. I also remained hypervigilant with respect to everything about my body; even a gurgle in my stomach would get my attention and stoke my anxiety. But because I had done so well, it was now safe to feel some of the fear that I had chased away before the surgery.

As I'd so often guided my patients, I was ready to lead myself on a course through my fears, taking them one by one, in relation to my present and future time frames, considering my best- and worst-case scenarios and the most realistic assessment of my new situation.

In my most dreaded configuration, I was unrealistically vulnerable, facing a worsening illness and impending handicaps. In my most idealized version of the future, I was unrealistically invulnerable, totally restored and never to be sick again. The realistic middle ground was most useful in priming my central awareness: I was not about to keel over lifeless. Although I was not immune to any future illnesses, I was, however, basically recovered, strong, competent, and able to be fully active again. I was also looking after myself and caring for others and my work.

Even more important, I was able to turn my gaze outward, appreciating how good it felt to be able to depend and to rely on others, knowing that their caring for me cost them time, effort, and anxious concern. Throughout the more difficult times, I gratefully surrendered to the expertise of the health-care teams and to the sympathy and compassion of family and friends. I know I am a lucky man—and also a happy one.

❦ Teaching Points ❦

If you are facing any kind of chronic illness or disabling condition, it is especially helpful to revamp your perspective as you enter the eye of the storm. Managing your responses to the situation will give you a fighting chance to restore happiness. Here are some useful tips:

- Make "Be prepared" your motto. Avoid being overly suspiciousness or hypervigilent and steer clear of protracted states of insulating yourself from awareness in which you disavow or deny what is likely to happen.
- Look out for and counteract ideas that might be so inappropriate that they impede your ability to create new ways of coping with adversity.
- Bring your self-image up-to-date and realistically emphasize your current strengths, coping ability, and innate worth as a human being, even if you are disabled and need to rely upon others.
- Face quickly and directly any hostile responses, irritability, and bitterness. Above all, don't verbally abuse your helpers and comforters. Use your angry impulses as signals that there is work you may have to do to adapt to new circumstances.
- Expressing your anger at fate will not make a frustrating situation go away. Instead, plan how to stay

as safe as you can in meeting it. Brace yourself but
also "brace up" without despair or giving up.

- Look for elements of choice that maintain your
  sense of control. Having less control in the present
  than in the past should not be exaggerated into "I
  have no control whatsoever."
- Look for every possible silver lining in the dark
  clouds that may surround you. Use any available satisfactions to counteract the drain on your
  energy.

Multnomah County Library

503.988.5123
multcolib.org

09/22/2018

Items checked out to   p12988534

A course in happiness : mastering

31168095176275

DUE DATE   10-13-18

___

Jack Kerouac and Allen Ginsberg :

31168103891980

DUE DATE   10-13-18

___

Ten Activities That Might Make You Happier

Throughout this book, you've been learning all about the major pathways to happiness by increasing your capacity for integration, intimacy, and integrity. You've almost completed the course. The last lesson is that, aside from all the work of personal growth that's required for inner harmony of the long-lasting variety, there are brief periods of enjoyment that are also an important element of happiness. There are numerous things that happen in our day-to-day lives that bring us laughter and light-heartedness. These are the golden nuggets of richness we pick up along the way as we grow into wiser, kinder, and more loving selves.

1. Savor Pleasurable Sensations and Satisfy Your Appetites
This statement seems obvious, doesn't it? Of course, it feels good to seek pleasurable moments, but true success in doing so lies in your timing and in understanding your responsibility to yourself and others.

As a medical student, I ate jelly doughnuts with powdered sugar every morning, a candy bar at midafternoon, and more chocolate at midnight. I don't do that anymore. Now, my priorities—to be healthy and fit—trump my sweet tooth these days (except for the occasional chocolate indulgence).

The goal for all of us is to enjoy healthy, positive pleasures. If satisfaction of a particular appetite leads to distress, pain, or suffering for you or someone else, you've missed the point. *Reflection* is the watchword.

Many of us place obstacles in our own way. Sometimes we overplan or we are so strict with ourselves we can lead lives that are too arid, restrictive, or depressing. Expecting too much or too little can be a setup for inevitable disappointment. Again, reflect, and steer your thoughts toward the rational middle ground.

2. Enjoy Group Membership, Rituals, and Festivals

Many of us derive joy from being part of a group with common values. Celebrating a shared past and teaching our children a tradition to perpetuate is a frequent pleasure at holidays, birthdays, anniversaries, and graduations. Even televised events such as the Super Bowl, the Academy Awards, or political elections can create cherished memories of togetherness for families and friends.

Becoming an active part of a group can require foresight and planning, but they are worth the effort, even though group interaction is not always pleasant. Sometimes it can be annoying to be around others. We want to get close; then we want to get away. This push/pull is a common experience. Good social skills include tolerance for irritating differences and the ability to recognize and deal with our own fears of rejection or exploitation.

Significant differences will always exist between individuals within any group. We can all give off a wrong signal at the wrong time. Developing the ability to translate the intentions of others, forgive missteps, and grant others leeway is important in achieving the feeling of warm togetherness we all long for.

Some people consider themselves rebels, loners, and/or haters of what they call "group-think" and avoid all types of mixed social interaction. This attitude could be the result of a lack of self-confidence and/or the fear of shame, humiliation, and rejection—all aspects of excessively dreaded scenario thinking. Or it might also be a well-integrated individual's thoughtful choice based on personality and temperament. Knowing the difference is the measure of emotional health.

3. Embrace Diversity with Affectionate Regard

Not all social rewards occur in intimate connections. Sometimes it's pleasurable simply to be among people we don't know. I call it "observing the human parade," or "communing from a distance." Airports, buses, and subways can be stressful venues, but people watching anywhere can be engaging and interesting, help pass the time, take your mind off your self, and let you enjoy the moment.

Sometimes, we're tempted to criticize others excessively. We harbor unfair expectations of how people "should" behave. Being aware of this tendency and try-ing to curb it is good for your character and personal growth. When I realize I'm being critical or judgmental, my commandment to myself is: *Thou shall not be repelled by differences.* In a public place, think of yourself as being on an anthropological field trip. Enjoy what Buddha called "benevolent detachment."

Self-consciousness can be an obstacle to this simple activ-ity of people watching in public. Comparing yourself with others is a tricky proposition. People like to look at people. We interest each other in a distant, visual sense, without wanting to become intimate, and it's healthy for all of us to know and accept this. If you are fearful of public humilia-tion or of being discomforted by the sense that all eyes are on you, judging, take it as a signal there is some inner work to be done. Once you accept the task, you are on your way to overcoming the problem and being free of it forever.

4. Allow Time for Peace, Quiet, and Solitude

Is coming home to the couch, TV set, a quick meal, and a favorite drink emotionally healthy for you? Yes, if you're actively enjoying having a rest. No, if you're only escap-ing from life that could contain more satisfactions in action. Again, knowing the difference is all-important for true happiness.

Solitude can be pleasant and restorative, an opportu-nity to revel in your own rhythm. And it can be a time to escape, not only from the noise of the world but also from the noisy inner world of intrusive thoughts.

Unfinished business tends to come unbidden into the

mind. Hardest of all is unfinished business from traumatic memories and current crises. You *can*, methodically and deliberately, set time aside during which you refuse to deal with these issues. Remembering Scarlett O'Hara's famous line in *Gone With the Wind* may help: *I'll think about that tomorrow*, you might say to yourself. It's good to develop an attitude that allows you *not* to have to check off everything on the to-do list. The intrusion may occur, but you can develop a mental set to let it go *for the time being*. This gives you control of a dose-by-dose approach to contemplating hard topics and choices.

Perfectionism and workaholism both support the idea that we need to be productive in every waking moment but it does *not* make for a healthy lifestyle. Enjoying relaxation without being fretful and achieving balance in all areas of your life—even allowing yourself to procrastinate now and then—is important for living well.

5. Enjoy Your Achievement, Status, and Power in Work, and Your Competence in Your Creative Pursuits

One of the goals of integration is to accept yourself as a skillful and talented person. That doesn't mean you have to have reached the pinnacle. There will always be those who are better at your game than you are. Keep at it. Being absorbed in something that stretches but does not overwhelm you is a very good situation to be in. Happiness can be associated with a sense of slow, steady improvement in whatever you choose to do.

One obstacle to taking pride in yourself is comparing your realistic self-appraisal to idealized expectations of yourself—a surefire setup for disappointment. Another obstacle is the opposite: being too proud, showing off, becoming arrogant and abrasive. If you strut, become vain, or complain that you are less admired than you deserve, you will alienate others. So, evaluate your skills and gifts truthfully, in a manner that keeps you on good terms with the rest of the world *and* yourself.

6. Appreciate the Achievements of Others

You are not alone and need never be bored if you can derive joy from the achievements of others, not only in the present but also in the historical development of our civilization. Exploring architecture, literature, music, art, film, dance, sport, and all other forms of human expression means that in a lifetime you will never run out of moments to be informed, enlightened, awed, and touched.

Jealousy, envy, grandiosity, and a sense of personal entitlement can be obstacles to these rich sources of enjoyment. If you find yourself in a mud trap, then slog out. You'll be glad you did.

7. Enjoy Excitement and the Mastery of Threats

Some of us feel most alive when we flirt with danger. So whether you like the challenge of mountain climbing, hunting, white-water rafting, flying, parachuting, racing, wrestling, ice fishing, scuba diving, or lifting tons of weight, it is your choice. Being able to triumph in the face of physical danger can be exhilarating. Yet, if you go too far, you can damage yourself. So once again it is important to plan what you want and to keep it within advisable limits.

I love to take people sailing in my small boat on San Francisco Bay. In summer, there are often high winds due to the fog banks that roll in. When this happens, the boat leans over with the power of the wind in the sail and forges through choppy waves. To the inexperienced, it feels as if the boat will tip over at any moment. It won't, of course; it has the safety feature of a heavy keel, invisible below the water. Some people do not like this thrill. They prefer the pleasant sensations that come with soft winds, and they like to join me during spring and fall, when the sun and waves caress the boat, allowing gentle movement through what one of my kids calls "creamy filling."

Some people recklessly seek increasingly greater and greater hazards, just to maintain a maximum level of exhilaration. Recently, I read about two very experienced recreational sailors from my dock area who went out to sea in a race, despite extremely dangerous weather conditions. The waves were fifteen feet tall and the wind over thirty mph in an area known for unpredictability. The wreckage of their vessel was found two days later, and the body of one of the sailors had washed ashore.

So consider your choices carefully, weighing your thrills against the risk. This applies to physical dangers as well as emotional ones, such as the risk of a broken heart.

8. Embrace Your Soul and Spirit

Most people have an intuitive sense of spiritual matters. Personal spiritual paths can range from a deep and disciplined involvement with an organized religion to experiences of periodic feelings of meaning and even to an oceanic sense of being beyond a limiting envelope of self.

Intellectualism and rationality disrupt such states. Getting caught up in excessively logical philosophizing destroys the simple pleasure of feeling in a state of grace. This state of mind is not based on science. It is purely subjective and fleeting. Faith can bring comfort, reassurance, forgiveness, and support when it is needed. Its value should not be underestimated.

Yet religion can also be detrimental and misguided. Here in Northern California we have quite a reputation for experimentation with various types of spirituality. In fact, many people devote enormous amounts of time to practices that they hope will bring them to a higher plane. This can turn out to be quite disappointing. For example, an acquaintance of mine entered a retreat and embraced a lifestyle of sleep deprivation and insufficient nutrition to meditate for several months. He left in his wake several unhappy children and a very angry spouse. When he emerged, he was more depressed than when he started.

Soulful pursuits are best looked upon as time well spent or as a journey rather than as a path to an ultimate and permanent state of immortality, omnipotence, or invulnerability to ordinary human suffering.

9. Make Efforts to Change the World for the Better

One of the most gratifying activities involves enhancing and enriching the lives of others. Many teens declare a wish to change the world for the better as their number-one goal in life. By adulthood, these young people often feel disillusioned.

I once knew a twenty-year-old who was taking many drugs. I asked him about his purposes for his life. He told me he had picketed to protest the Vietnam War, but the government would not stop it, so he gave up. He had wanted to improve things, expected far too much, and used the disappointment as an excuse to abandon his values. Like him, there are others who have also given up on society and reverted to making a lot of money. Some even gained power, but rather than use it for good, they were corrupted by it.

Excessively high expectations can trip us up. The ideal goal for making changes appears on one of my favorite bumper stickers: *Think globally, act locally.* Enjoy what you *can* do.

Any legacy that you might leave through your work to improve the world has incalculable value: planting a tree, helping to get a law passed, giving one person a feeling of being well cared for. Reducing the distress of others in any small way can make many moments happier for you. It can provide you with pride, a stronger sense of self-worth, and an enhanced view of yourself. It can also help mend your own grievances about not having received enough, bringing more kindness, which we all want, into the world.

10. Enjoy the Flow of Generations

If we were not a procreative species, we would be extinct. We are hardwired to be drawn to new birth. But enjoyment of the flow of generations does not mean only appreciating the children or grandchildren in your own family. Embracing renewal encompasses finding pleasure in seeing any children at play, or in passing on a skill or bit of wisdom to any younger individual, or in watching new kittens play, or even in noting the replanting of trees in a cut forest. Let these events, wherever you find them, bring you joy.

This can be a daunting task. Sometimes, in our pain over our own hardships and lost chances, we harbor bitterness at the unlimited potential of the young. Or our expectations for the next generation are idealized: *These kids will fulfill all our goals and dreams for them*, we think. Which, of course, is a type of best-case–scenario thinking that can catch us if we're not alert to it.

Simple pleasures are available to us all the time, each and every day. This is true wherever we each happen to be on our journey to knowing our self, to recognizing our true values and priorities, and to enjoying a genuine connection to people, community, and the earth.

ACKNOWLEDGMENTS

My happiness was constructed in a life filled with love with Renée Binder, who helped me organize the fundamental scaffolding of this work and participated in every aspect of its process and completion. Her experiences as a psychotherapist also amplified the illustrative stories. My agent, Andrea Hurst, guided me through both writing a proposal and getting a contract; great gratitude goes to her. She put me in contact with Sara Carder of Tarcher/Penguin, who was invariably encouraging and wise. I am deeply indebted to the outstanding skills of Lee Quarfoot for her optimism, ideas, close-in commentary, and editing as I composed the entire manuscript. She was uplifting, as befits this topic, and came up with some crucial reorganizing concepts!

I began this book as a series of ideas discussed during her terminal illness with my former wife Carol Horowitz. It was so splendid that she found it meaningful and pleasant to read and correct some of my writing. Then the book went on hold for a bit, until Renée helped me reach its present conceptual frame. During the process,

I read segments to family and friends. Jordan and Janet Horowitz, Josh Horowitz, Ariana Strozzi, Craig Peters, Maureen DuBour, Mark Peters, Sara Reba, and Steven Walsh were especially helpful.

Margarite Salinas, my administrative assistant, was unflagging in processing the many versions as I "transmogrified" my basic material into what you hold in your hands. While her word processing was terrific, her attitude was even more sustaining during periods of doubting. *Thanks again to all.*

MARDI HOROWITZ
San Francisco, August 2008

A Summary of Tools and Techniques Discussed in This Book

Here are brief notes on the techniques discussed in this book.

1. Center attention on self and try to harmonize what you find.
Use the Three Scenarios Approach.

1. What are your idealized goals?
2. What things do you dread most when you think of the future?
3. What do you choose as realistic now and desirable future aims?

2. Do not give up or give in.
You come back to reflecting on yourself by using a dose-by-dose approach. Keep a list of your characteristics and attributes. Revise the list, adding some and deleting

others. Look out for exaggerated negatives, grandiose positives, and outmoded beliefs.

3. Make new choices and plan new actions.

Separate out what you think of yourself here and now from what you used to think of yourself when you were overly influenced by others.

4. Jump over hurdles.

There will be obstacles to your efforts at self-review. Try to list some of these. Name the beasts by giving each difficult topic some kind of a label. This will help you deal with the topic multiple times, gaining clarity as you go along.

5. Get into the right frame of mind to consider any difficult topic.

Instead of warding off stressful topics and then having them pop up unbidden into your mind, you are going to bid them to enter your mind during a state of calm contemplation. This means preparing your mind to slowly think about emotional ideas. It means you will keep rage, fear, guilt, shame, and sadness within a range where you are not acting impulsively, thinking irrationally, or feeling overwhelmed by an intense mood.

6. Focus attention.

The most likely topics that you will choose to contemplate are a troublesome memory from your past, a frustrating relationship in the present, or a difficult but pending future choice. These stressful and emotional themes may be blocking your progress in deciding how to move forward in self-reconceptualization. Focus on what they mean to you now.

7. Aim at rational decision-making.

Most likely you will hope to arrive at some useful conclusion, one that you can remember and that you can reclaim again when the topic returns to your mind. But if your topic is a difficult one, you may not reach this conclusion in one sitting. The situation is like painting a complex portrait: You will need to confront your subject over several sittings. Sometimes writing down your appraisals after each "session" is helpful. This path toward completion is a "dose-by-dose" approach: Like a loaf of bread, you take it one slice at a time until you are done. I once saw a button printed with "Don't be too sure" pinned on the lapel of a teaching physician's white coat. Do not fix your first conclusion in amber; reconsider it later. This aim at mastery of a previously difficult topic is sometimes helped by remembering to use the Five *R*s:

- Reconsider: Review the topic again.
- Reperceive: Retell the story.
- Reappraise: Separate out probable realities from projections from within.
- Revise: Evaluate pros and cons, then alter your plan for coping and seeking satisfaction.
- Rehearse: Practice your new plan in your mind, recheck, and implement it at the right time.

8. Clarify dilemmas.

As you reflect upon your intimate relationships, you will encounter patterns that do not work as well as you would like. You can begin to unpack these patterns by telling a story about a specific instance. As you go back to the memories, clarify what happened and then consider how and why each episode in a cause-and-effect sequence occurred. What actions led to what consequences? Who did what to whom? Why and how did emotional responses and reactions occur?

You may be snagged in a dilemma: You can move right, but that will cause trouble. So you move to the left, but, oh no, that causes some other trouble. This is a "damned if I do/damned if I don't" situation. These dilemmas are about self-goals, we-goals, and the goals of and for significant others that as such are worth analyzing slowly.

Try to weed out the parts that are not as beneficial and rearrange them. Consider your actions and the reactions of others. How are you likely to respond to their reactions? See if jotting down notes helps. Write down your or their action, then their or your response, followed by your or their reactions. You can even fill in the blanks of sentences such as "If I do _____ then the other person will _____, and then I am likely to feel _____ because _____ and so _____."

9. For your most important attachments, consider best- and worst-case as well as realistic scenarios.
The action, response, and reaction model ends with feelings of evaluation or even criticism. These emotions

include how you might feel in a range from self-esteem to self-disgust. Evaluate these feelings. Examine your most ideal and most dreaded extremes. Then examine the more realistic, middle-of-the-road scenarios. That is, consider the best/worst anticipated outcome and your more reasonable expectations.

Try to see the differences between expectations and new opportunities. Reconsider the roles and character-istics you expect others to take. Are these accurate or merely your projections? How about the roles you assign to yourself? Pay special attention to any too grand or too incompetent roles.

10. Contemplate interpersonal dilemmas with integrity.
Many dilemmas involve morality, ethics, and personal values, and most of us prefer blaming others rather than ourselves. Taking responsibility is sometimes a useful way out of "blame games" that merely project personal faults onto others. If you are deceitful, reconsider your values. You may need to take more responsibility for future choices. The adage "fool me once, shame on you; fool me twice, shame on me" means that we should learn from our experiences and not submit to future repetitions of another person's abuse or deceitfulness.

In deciding whether to keep a relationship or break it off, it is helpful to consider both your traits and those of the other person. Ask these three questions, to get an idea of what to expect in the future of such a relationship. Ask them of both yourself *and* the other person.

- How *consistent* is this person in manifesting the virtue of honesty?
- How *reliable* is each person in the virtue of doing what they say they will do, and mean to do?
- How *competent* is each person in being likely to accomplish the tasks they must take on to maintain a good relationship?

If you are incompetent, don't promise to do more than you can. If you are unreliable, find out why.

When you see traits you do not like in a loved one, it causes you distress; if you see such traits in yourself, you may feel guilt or shame. You won't like such feelings—who would?—but since they are there, use them to motivate yourself to change for the better.

See if you can tolerate negative feelings to a greater extent than you could when you were younger. Back then you avoided considerations that activated too much distress, anxiety, sadness, shame, and guilt. Now that you have the wherewithal to confront such emotions, you can afford to look at the ideas you once repressed in order to avoid these strong feelings.

11. Prioritize your own values.
Look for competing values. Which good thing is better than what other good thing? If in doubt, err on the side of kindness, compassion, letting go of resentments or excessive "obligations," and practicing forgiveness rather than on the side of isolation, self-service, perfectionism, and

12. Look out for traps.

Traps include excessive perfectionism, procrastination, self-righteousness, and self-pity. Your habitual traps will snare you again and again, but everyone makes "human errors." Look out for demoralization; it is a transient mood. Rest, unsnag yourself, and come back to the topic when you can be hopeful again.

13. Provide some self-encouragement.

How can you reinforce or reward yourself?

14. Repeat hopeful, rational routes to more satisfaction.

Rehearse good plans in your imagination. Only by repetition will a new way of acting in the world become your own automatic style. New patterns may feel awkward at first, but poise and confidence will ultimately grow.

By repeating your efforts on different themes you will learn about yourself (integration), your most vital connections (intimacy), and the principles that you live by (integrity). You will also learn how to learn and how to think through hard topics, as summarized in the following outline.

METHODS FOR WORKING ON
A HARD TOPIC

1. Select a hard topic to contemplate and work on:
   a. one that has a tendency to often intrude into your mind

b. one that gives you pangs of intense and confusing emotions, a medley of feelings you intuitively know you should "unpack"

c. one that keeps you from making good plans for moving on

2. Then get in the right frame of mind:
   a. Create a calm state where you can give yourself time to proceed slowly.
   b. Establish an intention to think "clear and fresh" while avoiding harsh self-criticism.
   c. Aim at thinking as well as thinking about how you are thinking.

3. Next, set goals that you hope to achieve from your period of contemplation:
   a. Move forward and remember your key ideas.
   b. Use dose-by-dose thinking rather than expect that you will come up with an absolute solution in just one session.
   c. Plan to "not be too sure" about your conclusions in a given session; have an open mind.

4. Clarify the various aspects of a topic:
   a. Write down the ideas, feelings, and values associated with a topic.

b. Establish cause and effect.

c. Consider what is preventing you from moving forward.

5. Expand the topic's meanings:
   a. Include your intentions and expectations.
   b. Describe the intentions and expectations of others.
   c. Include your reactions to their intentions and expectations.

6. Examine contexts and scenarios of what is likely and unlikely to happen:
   a. best (idealized) versions
   b. worst (dreaded or catastrophic) versions
   c. more realistic (or middle-ground) versions

7. Separate reality from fantasy:
   a. Challenge your current appraisals with alternative ones.
   b. Reconsider the roles you use to organize what events mean to and about you.
   c. Be optimistic but rationally so. Do not give up or give in as a quick "way out."

8. Prioritize your own values:
   a. State your principles.
   b. Which are more important than others?
   c. Choose a path of gratitude, compassion, letting go, and forgiveness.

9. Make realistic decisions:

    a. Focus on plans for the near future, and then imagine their long-term implications.

    b. Imagine following these plans in various contexts.

    c. Practice new actions. (Expect them to feel awkward at first.)

SUPPLEMENTAL REFERENCES

Cloninger, C. R. *Feeling Good: The Science of Well Being* (New York: Oxford University Press, 2004).

Csikszentmihalyi, M. *Flow: The Psychology of Optimal Experience* (New York: HarperCollins, 1990).

Fava, G. A., and Ruini, C. "Development and characteristics of a well-being enhancing psychotherapeutic strategy: Well-being therapy." *Journal of Behavior Therapy and Experimental Psychiatry* 34 (2003): 45–63.

Fordyce, M. W. "A program to increase happiness: Further studies." *Journal of Counseling Psychology* 30 (1983): 483–98.

Fredrickson, B. L., and C. Branigan. "Positive emotions broaden the scope of attention and thought-action repertoires." *Cognition and Emotion* 19 (2005): 313–32.

Frisch, M. B. *Quality of Life Therapy: Applying a Life Satisfaction Approach to Positive Psychology and Cognitive Therapy* (Hoboken, NJ: Wiley, 2006).

Gilbert, D. *Stumbling Onto Happiness* (New York: Knopf, 2006).

Gottman, V. N. *The Seven Principles for Making Marriage Work* (New York: Three Rivers, 1999).

Haidt, A. *The Happiness Hypothesis* (New York: Basic Books, 2006).

Hendrix, H. *Getting the Love You Want* (New York: Holt, 1988).

Horowitz, M. J. *Cognitive Psychodynamics: From Conflict to Character* (New York: Wiley, 1998).

Joseph, S., and A. P. Linley. "Positive psychological approaches to therapy. *Counseling and Psychotherapy Research* 5 (2005): 5–10.

Karasu, T. B. *The Art of Serenity* (New York: Simon and Schuster, 2003).

Kushner, H. *Living a Life That Matters* (New York: Knopf, 2001).

Lear, J. *Happiness, Death, and the Remainder of Life* (Cambridge: Harvard University Press, 2000).

Lyubomirsky, S., K. M. Sheldon, and D. Schkade. "Pursuing happiness: The architecture of sustainable change." *Review of General Psychology* 9 (2005): 111–31.

Seligman, M. E. P. *Authentic Happiness: Using the New Positive Psychology to Realize Your Potential for Lasting Fulfillment* (New York: Free Press, 2002).

Seligman, M. E. P., T. A. Steen, N. Park, and C. Peterson. "Positive psychology progress: Empirical validation of interventions." *American Psychologist* 60 (2005): 410–21.

ABOUT THE AUTHOR

Mardi Horowitz is a professor of psychiatry at the University of California, San Francisco, School of Medicine, where, at Langley Porter Psychiatric Institute, he directs the Center on Stress and Personality. He is also president of San Francisco Center for Psychoanalysis, and recipient of the Lifetime Achievement Award of the International Society for Traumatic Stress Studies and the Distinguished Life Fellowship of the American Psychiatric Association. The latter organization also gave him the Foundation's Fund Prize for Research in Psychiatry, for his development of the diagnosis of post-traumatic stress disorder, as well as its Hibb's Award for his work on grief. Dr. Horowitz was asked by the American Psychotherapy Association Press to write *Understanding Psychotherapy Changes*. Among his other books are *Stress Response Syndromes*, now in its fourth edition, and *Cognitive Psychodynamics: From Conflict to Character*. He lives with his partner, Renée, and their dog, Romeo, in the San Francisco Bay area.